THE MUSIC-LOVER'S BIRTHDAY BOOK

THE METROPOLITAN MUSEUM OF ART

HARRY N. ABRAMS, INC., Publishers

New York

THIS BOOK was prepared in association with the Music Division of The New York Public Library Performing Arts Research Center at Lincoln Center. Special thanks are due to Jean Bowen and her staff for cheerfully guiding us through the diverse treasures in their collection and helping with the general research. Laurence Libin, Ken Moore, and the rest of the staff of the Museum's Department of Musical Instruments were particularly helpful, as was the Department of Prints and Photographs. All the illustrations in this book not otherwise marked are from the collections of The Metropolitan Museum of Art, photographed by the Museum's Photograph Studio. All New York Public Library pieces were photographed by Sheldan Collins.

Copyright © 1987 by The Metropolitan Museum of Art
All rights reserved
Produced by the Department of Special Publications,
The Metropolitan Museum of Art
Designed by Peter Oldenburg
Composition by Finn Typographic Service, Inc.
Printed and bound in Italy by Sagdos S.p.A.

ISBN 0-87099-494-8 MMA
ISBN 0-8109-1447-6 Abrams

PREFACE

THIS RECORD BOOK is a celebration of music and musicians. In it more than one thousand birthdays, from Claudio Abbado's to Teresa Zylis-Gara's, are noted. Divas and crooners, rock and blues singers, flamenco and country-western guitarists, composers of operas and musical comedies, and classical and jazz instrumentalists are gathered here in the company of instrument makers, conductors, critics, songwriters, patrons, publishers, musicologists, educators, lexicographers, and impresarios. Unexpected names appear along with the obvious. Because of their musical accomplishments, Albert Schweitzer (January 14), Henry VIII (June 28), and Friedrich Nietzsche (October 15) stand proudly alongside "Jelly Roll" Morton and Wolfgang Amadeus Mozart.

There are notable, though unavoidable, omissions. Early-music fans will miss the names of such musicians as Henry Purcell and Palestrina, who were born before reliable birth records were kept. Because our format allowed us to cite only three musicians each day, we were forced to exclude artists who deserve to be in this book. For example, despite the overabundance of talent born on December 16 – Ludwig van Beethoven, James McCracken, Sir Noel Coward, "Turk" Murphy, Zoltán Kodály, and Menahem Pressler – only three could be chosen. Sacrifices include Jim Croce (January 10), Sarah Caldwell and Julius Rudel (March 6), Rosemary Clooney (May 23), and Ignacy Jan Paderewski (November 18). And since some days mark the births of many well-known musicians and others of only a few, relatively minor artists are occasionally included and some renowned ones are not.

To confirm the spellings of the names and birth dates, we consulted *Baker's Biographical Dictionary of Musicians* (seventh edition), edited by Nicolas Slonimsky, and *The New Grove Dictionary of Music and Musicians* (1980), edited by Stanley Sadie. If birth dates conflicted, we used those given by Grove. When only baptismal dates were available, we used them. When controversy surrounds the birth date of a well-known artist, we chose the date that has come to be universally celebrated.

Surprising combinations occur throughout the book. For instance, two legendary masters of the violin, Fritz Kreisler and Jascha Heifetz, share February 2 as their birth date, while three celebrated singers – Joan Sutherland, Mary Travers, and Joni Mitchell – were born on November 7. The birthdays of the composers Johannes Brahms and Piotr Ilyich Tchaikovsky are celebrated on May 7; two conductors, Sir Thomas Beecham and Zubin Mehta, share April 29. And how fitting it seems that Stephen Foster, Louis Armstrong, and Mitch Miller – three men of quintessentially American music – were born on the Fourth of July.

Birthdays also produce some interesting juxtapositions: Gustav Mahler, Gian Carlo Menotti, and Ringo Starr are honored on July 7; "Leadbelly," Richie Havens, and Placido Domingo on January 21; George Frideric Handel and Johnny Winter on February 23.

Beneath each name we have included a brief note on the musician's nationality and the work for which he or she is best known. Our style has been to give the nationality at birth first, then any citizenship later adopted. Thus Kurt Weill is a "German-born American" composer and Vladimir Ashkenazy is a "Russian-born Icelandic" pianist. Thoughtful and amusing quotations appear throughout the book. You can read Richard Strauss on conducting, "Dizzy" Gillespie on Louis Armstrong, Samuel Johnson on fiddling, and Mark Twain on Wagner.

The art that appears throughout this book is as rich and varied as the musicians in it. Works have been drawn from the collections of The Metropolitan Museum of Art and The New York Public Library and reveal how profoundly music has influenced the sister arts for thousands of years: from a Cycladic statue of a harpist carved around 3000 B.C. to Fernando Botero's boisterous painting *Dancing in Colombia* of 1980; from a luminous painting by Vermeer to a plaintive watercolor by Thomas Eakins; from a mandolin decorated with tortoiseshell and ivory to Frank Lloyd Wright's elegant, spare design for a piano screen. The Music Division of The New York Public Library Performing Arts Research Center at Lincoln Center has contributed such pieces as spirited caricatures of Massenet, Koussevitzky, and Sousa; a touching drawing of Yehudi Menuhin as a little boy playing the violin; a whimsical self-portrait by Enrico Caruso; and many other treasures.

As you leaf through this book, looking for your favorite musicians and discovering those born on your birthday, you may begin to hum the cheering tune "Happy Birthday to You." Composed by Mildred Hill, it can be sung to *her* on June 27.

Alden Rockwell Murphy
Editor

THE MUSIC-LOVER'S BIRTHDAY BOOK

January 1

Robert De Cormier 1922
American composer, conductor, and arranger

Milt "Bags" Jackson 1923
American jazz vibraphonist, pianist, and guitarist

Eve Queler 1936
American conductor

January 2

Mily Balakirev 1837
Russian composer and collector of Russian music

Sir Michael Tippett 1905
British composer and librettist

Roger Miller 1936
American country-music singer, guitarist, and songwriter

January 3

Henriette Sontag 1806
German soprano

Victor Borge 1909
Danish pianist and comedic performer

Stephen Stills 1945
American rock guitarist and singer

January 4

Giovanni Battista Pergolesi 1710
Italian composer

Josef Suk 1874
Czech violinist and composer

Grace Bumbry 1937
American mezzo-soprano

January 5

Frederick Shepherd Converse 1871
American composer

Alfred Brendel 1931
Austrian pianist

Maurizio Pollini 1942
Italian pianist

January 6

Max Bruch 1838
German composer

Alexander Scriabin 1872
Russian composer

Earl Scruggs 1924
American country-music
singer, banjo player, and
songwriter

Concert
Umberto Brunelleschi, French, b. 1879
Illustration from *La Guirlande: Album d'Art et de
Littérature*
Paris, ca. 1920

Thomas J. Watson Library
The Metropolitan Museum of Art

All one's life is music, if one touches the notes rightly,
and in time.

John Ruskin

January 7

Francis Poulenc 1899
French composer

Jean-Pierre Rampal 1922
French flutist

Kenny Loggins 1948
American pop-rock singer,
songwriter, and guitarist

January 8

Hans von Bülow 1830
German pianist and conductor

Elvis Presley 1935
American rock-and-roll singer
and guitarist

David Bowie 1947
British rock singer, songwriter,
and actor

January 9

Sir Rudolf Bing 1902
Austrian-born British operatic
impresario

Joan Baez 1941
American folk singer, guitarist,
and songwriter

Crystal Gayle 1951
American country-music singer

January
10

Max Roach 1925
American jazz drummer

Sherrill Milnes 1935
American baritone

Rod Stewart 1945
British rock singer and
songwriter

January
11

Christian Sinding 1856
Norwegian composer

Reinhold Glière 1875
Russian composer

Maurice Duruflé 1902
French organist and composer

La Dame de Monte Carlo and **La Voix Humaine**
Music by Francis Poulenc, words by Jean Cocteau
Sheet-music covers by Jean Cocteau, French, 1889–1963
Color lithographs
Paris: S. A. Editions Ricordi, 1961 and 1959
  Music Division, The New York Public Library

Good music resembles something. It resembles the
composer.

Jean Cocteau

January 12

Ermanno Wolf-Ferrari 1876
Italian opera composer

Pierre Bernac 1899
French baritone

Jay McShann 1916
American jazz pianist, blues
singer, composer, and
bandleader

January 13

Heinrich Hofmann 1842
German pianist and composer

Sophie Tucker 1884
Russian-born American
burlesque and vaudeville singer

Laurence Powell 1899
British-born American
composer and conductor

January 14

Ludwig von Köchel 1800
Austrian musicographer; compiler of the Mozart catalogue

Albert Schweitzer 1875
Alsatian humanitarian, physician, Bach scholar, and organist

Louis Quilico 1929
Canadian baritone

Barrel Piano with Dancing Figures
George Hicks, American, b. ca. 1818, d. 1863
Wood and various other materials, ca. 1860
The Crosby Brown Collection of Musical Instruments, 1889   89.4.2048

There's a barrel-organ carolling across a
    golden street,
In the city as the sun sinks low;
And the music's not immortal; but the world
    has made it sweet
And fulfilled it with the sunset glow.

Alfred Noyes

January 15

Gene Krupa 1909
American jazz bandleader and drummer

Elie Siegmeister 1909
American composer

Chuck Berry 1926
American rock-and-roll singer, songwriter, and guitarist

January 16

Ethel Merman 1908
American singer of popular music

Marilyn Horne 1929
American mezzo-soprano

Katia Ricciarelli 1946
Italian soprano

L'Art Céleste
Odilon Redon, French, 1840–1916
Lithograph, 1894
  Gift of A. W. Bahr, 1958   58.547.26

Enough of clouds, waves, aquariums, water-sprites and
nocturnal scents; what we need is a music of the earth,
everyday music . . . music one can live in like a house.

Jean Cocteau

François-Joseph Gossec 1734
  Belgian composer

Henk Badings 1907
  Dutch composer

Donald Erb 1927
  American composer

César Cui 1835
  Russian composer

Emmanuel Chabrier 1841
  French composer

January
19

Phil Everly 1939
American rock-and-roll singer
and guitarist

Janis Joplin 1943
American blues-rock singer and
songwriter

Dolly Parton 1946
American country-music singer
and songwriter

January
20

Ernest Chausson 1855
French composer

Walter Piston 1894
American composer

David Tudor 1926
American pianist and composer
of experimental music

You can't teach a young musician to compose any
more than you can teach a delicate plant to grow,
but you can guide him a little by putting a stick in
here and a stick in there.

Frederick Delius

The Haydn Sonata
Margery Austen Ryerson, American, b. 1886
Etching
Gift of William M. Lybrand, 1942   42.33.29

LE JAZZOFLUTE
ROBE DU SOIR, DE BEER

January
21

Huddie "Leadbelly" Ledbetter 1885
American blues guitarist, folk
singer, and songwriter

Placido Domingo 1941
Spanish tenor and conductor

Richie Havens 1941
American rock singer

Le Jazzoflute
Georges Lepape, French, 1887–1971
Illustration from *Gazette du Bon Ton: Arts, Modes &
Frivolités*, 1922
Paris: Librairie Centrale des Beaux-Arts

Thomas J. Watson Library
The Metropolitan Museum of Art

The flute is not an instrument with a good moral effect. It
is too exciting.

Aristotle

Extraordinary how potent cheap music is.

Sir Noel Coward

January 22

John J. Becker 1886
American composer

Rosa Ponselle 1897
American soprano

Sam Cooke 1935
American rhythm-and-blues
singer

January 23

Muzio Clementi 1752
Italian pianist and composer

Teresa Zylis-Gara 1937
Polish soprano

January 24

Norman Dello Joio 1913
American composer

Leon Kirchner 1919
American composer and pianist

Neil Diamond 1941
American pop-rock singer and
songwriter

You better get me something good in Bali.

January 25

Wilhelm Furtwängler 1886
German conductor and
composer

Witold Lutoslawski 1913
Polish composer

January 26

Stéphane Grappelli 1908
French jazz violinist

Eartha Kitt 1928
American singer of popular music

Jacqueline DuPré 1945
British cellist

January 27

Wolfgang Amadeus Mozart 1756
Austrian composer

Edouard Lalo 1823
French composer

Jerome Kern 1885
American songwriter and composer of musical comedies

January 28

Ferdinand Hérold 1791
French composer

Artur Rubinstein 1887
Polish-born American pianist

John Tavener 1944
British avant-garde composer

Whether the angels play only Bach in praising God I am not quite sure: I am sure, however, that *en famille* they play Mozart.

Karl Barth

O Mozart, immortal Mozart, how many, how infinitely many inspiring suggestions of a finer, better life have you left in our souls!

Franz Schubert

The Magic Flute
Set design for the entrance of the Queen of the Night
Karl Friedrich Thiele, active 1780–1836, after Karl Friedrich Schinkel, German, 1781–1841
Hand- and plate-colored aquatint, 1819
The Elisha Whittelsey Collection, The Elisha Whittelsey Fund, 1954   54.602.1 (14)

January 29

Daniel-François-Esprit Auber 1782
French composer, primarily of comic operas

Frederick Delius 1862
British composer

Luigi Nono 1924
Italian composer

January 30

Charles Martin Loeffler 1861
Alsatian-born American composer

Walter Johannes Damrosch 1862
German conductor and composer

Lynn Harrell 1944
American cellist

January 31

Franz Schubert 1797
Austrian composer

Philip Glass 1937
American composer of minimalist music

Phil Collins 1951
British rock drummer, songwriter, and singer

Victor Herbert
Ralph Barton, American, 1891–1931
Caricature in pen and ink

Jascha Heifetz
Benedict F. Dolbin, Austrian, 1883–1971
Pencil

occasionally play works by contemporary composers
and for two reasons. First, to discourage the composer
from writing any more, and secondly to remind myself
how much I appreciate Beethoven.

Jascha Heifetz

February 1

Francesco Stradivari 1671
Italian violin maker

Victor Herbert 1859
Irish-born American conductor,
cellist, and composer of light music

Don Everly 1937
American rock-and-roll singer,
songwriter, and guitarist

February 2

Fritz Kreisler 1875
Austrian-born American violinist
and composer

Jascha Heifetz 1901
Russian-born American violinist

Stan Getz 1927
American jazz tenor saxophonist

Letter to Fanny Mendelssohn:

I have grown accustomed to composing in our garden . . .
today or tomorrow I am going to dream there the *Midsummer Night's Dream.*

Felix Mendelssohn

Letter from Scotland
Letter from Felix Mendelssohn, probably to his father,
Abraham Mendelssohn, dated August, 1, 1929,
written while the composer was beginning a tour of
the Scottish Highlands. The scene depicted in his
letter shows the harbor of Edinburgh.

Music Division, The New York Public Library

Still Life with Guitar and Music
Pablo Picasso, Spanish, 1881–1973
Color stencil, ca. 1920
Gift of Paul J. Sachs, 1922   22.86.6

The melody is generally what the piece is about.

Aaron Copland

February
5

Jussi Björling 1911
Swedish tenor

Sir John Pritchard 1921
British conductor

Bob Marley 1945
Jamaican reggae singer and
songwriter

February
6

Claudio Arrau 1903
Chilean pianist

Eubie Blake 1883
American jazz pianist, vaudevillian, songwriter, and composer

Oscar Brand 1920
Canadian folk singer and folklorist

Stuart Burrows 1933
Welsh tenor

February
8

John Williams 1932
American composer and conductor

Elly Ameling 1934
Dutch soprano

Tom Rush 1941
American folk singer, songwriter, and guitarist

February
9

Alban Berg 1885
Austrian composer

Hildegard Behrens 1937
German soprano

Carole King 1941
American pop-rock singer and songwriter

ver look at the trombones. It only encourages them.

Richard Strauss

vitation to the Sideshow (La Parade) (detail)
orges Pierre Seurat, French, 1859–1891
 on canvas, 1887–88
Bequest of Stephen C. Clark, 1960   61.101.17

February 10

Leontyne Price 1927
American soprano

Roberta Flack 1940
American pop-soul singer

Peter Allen 1944
Australian pop singer, songwriter, and pianist

February 11

Rudolf Firkušný 1912
Czech-born American pianist

Edith Mathis 1938
Swiss soprano

Sergio Mendes 1941
Brazilian jazz pianist and composer

February 12

Roy Harris 1898
American composer

Mel Powell 1923
American jazz pianist and composer

February 13

Feodor Chaliapin 1873
Russian bass

"Tennessee" Ernie Ford 1919
American country-music singer and songwriter

Eileen Farrell 1920
American soprano

February 14

Pier Francesco Cavalli 1602
Italian composer

Alexander Dargomyzhsky 1813
Russian composer

Ignaz Friedman 1882
Polish pianist and composer

February 15

Michael Praetorius 1571
German organist, composer,
and theorist

Heinrich Engelhard Steinway 1797
German piano manufacturer

Harold Arlen 1905
American composer of musicals
and songs

Japanese Acrobat Playing a Samisen
Detail of a handscroll painted in ink and colors
on paper
Japanese, 18th–19th century, Edo period
Gift of Mrs. Henry J. Bernheim, 1945   45.97.5

My idea is that there is music in the air, music all around
us, the world is full of it and you simply take as much as
you require.

Sir Edward Elgar

February 16

David Mannes 1866
American violinist and conductor; founder of the Mannes College of Music

Alec Wilder 1907
American composer, arranger, and songwriter

John Corigliano 1938
American composer

February 17

Arcangelo Corelli 1653
Italian violinist and composer

Marian Anderson 1902
American contralto

"Buddy" De Franco 1923
American jazz clarinetist and bandleader

February 18

Pietro Giovanni Guarneri 1655
Italian violin maker

Sir George Henschel 1850
German-born British conductor, composer, and baritone

Yoko Ono 1933
Japanese-born American rock singer, songwriter, and artist

February 19

Luigi Boccherini 1743
Italian composer

Stan Kenton 1912
American jazz pianist, composer, and bandleader

"Smokey" Robinson 1940
American rhythm-and-blues singer and songwriter

February 20

Carl Czerny 1791
  Austrian pianist and composer

Nancy Wilson 1937
  American jazz singer

Christoph Eschenbach 1940
  German pianist and conductor

February 21

Léo Delibes 1836
  French composer

Andrés Segovia 1893
  Spanish guitarist

Nina Simone 1933
  American jazz and soul singer

On Marian Anderson:

. . . a voice such as
one hears once in a
hundred years.

Arturo Toscanini

Marian Anderson
In the role of Ulrica in Verdi's
Un Ballo in Maschera
Richard Avedon, American, b. 1923
Gelatin-silver print, 1955

February 22

Niels Gade 1817
Danish composer

David Ahlstrom 1927
American composer

February 23

George Frideric Handel 1685
German-born English composer

Johnny Winter 1944
American blues-rock singer,
guitarist, and songwriter

February 24

Arrigo Boito 1842
Italian opera composer, librettist,
and poet

Arnold Dolmetsch 1858
British music antiquarian and
musician

Renata Scotto 1934
Italian soprano

On Handel:

Handel understands effect better than any of us—
when he chooses, he strikes like a thunderbolt.

Wolfgang Amadeus Mozart

He is the master of us all.   *Franz Joseph Haydn*

Handel, to him I bow the knee.   *Ludwig van Beethoven*

Handel Concerto
Esther Williams, American, 1907–196
Oil on canvas, 1935
George A. Hearn Fund, 1939   39.106

Rink Waltz
Sheet-music cover (detail)
Color lithograph
Detroit: J. Henry Whittemore & Co., 1868

Harris Brisbane Dick and Rogers Funds, The Elisha
Whittelsey Collection, The Elisha Whittelsey Fund and
Gift of John Size, by exchange, 1958   58.635.16 (27)

We are not an aria country. We are a song country.

Alan Jay Lerner

The Chaplet: A Waltz — Flora
Sheet-music cover
Color lithograph, 1829–33
Philadelphia: R. H. Hobson

Music Division, The New York Public Library

Dame Myra Hess 1890
British pianist

George Harrison 1943
British rock singer, guitarist, and
songwriter

February 26

"Fats" Domino 1928
American rock-and-roll pianist
and singer

Lazar Berman 1930
Soviet pianist

Johnny Cash 1932
American country-music singer,
guitarist, and songwriter

February 27

Enrico Caruso 1873
Italian tenor

Dexter Gordon 1923
American jazz tenor saxophonist

Mirella Freni 1935
Italian soprano

Self-Portrait
Enrico Caruso, Italian, 1873–1921
Pencil
Music Division, The New York Public Library

On Caruso:

In the glorious radiance of its timbre, in the life-giving
abundance of its tone, and in its plenitude and virility,
his voice seemed something inexhaustible. The capacity
for giving pleasure by Caruso was equaled by no other
figure of his time in all the realm of music.

Irving Kolodin

The man was unique. There never was a sound like his:
that heroic attack, that velvet suavity, that sheer, exultant
joy in singing.

Harold C. Schonberg

February 28

John Alden Carpenter 1876
American composer

Geraldine Farrar 1882
American soprano

Seymour Shifrin 1926
American composer

February 29

Gioachino Rossini 1792
Italian composer

Wladimir Vogel 1896
Russian-born Swiss composer

Jimmy Dorsey 1904
American clarinetist and
saxophonist

March 1

Frédéric Chopin 1810
Polish composer and pianist

Glenn Miller 1904
American trombonist and bandleader

Harry Belafonte 1927
American calypso and folk singer

March 2

Bedřich Smetana 1824
Bohemian composer

Kurt Weill 1900
German-born American composer of
operas and other music

Marc Blitzstein 1905
American composer

hopin
otéro Cosme, Brazilian
Woodcut, ca. 1940
Gift of Sotéro Cosme, 1944   44.28.9

ach is like an astronomer who, with the help of ciphers,
nds the most wonderful stars. . . . Beethoven embraced
he universe with the power of his spirit. . . . I do not
limb so high. A long time ago I decided that my universe
ill be the soul and heart of man.

Frédéric Chopin

March
3

Frank Wigglesworth 1918
American composer

Douglas Leedy 1938
American composer, pianist, and
conductor

Florence Quivar 1944
American mezzo-soprano

March
4

Antonio Vivaldi 1678
Italian composer

Samuel Adler 1928
German-born American composer

Bernard Haitink 1929
Dutch conductor

March
5

Arthur Foote 1853
American composer

Heitor Villa-Lobos 1887
Brazilian composer and
collector of Brazilian folk songs

Barry Tuckwell 1931
Australian French-horn player

Musical Clown
Alexander Zerdin Kruse, American, 1890–1972
Lithograph
Gift of The Weyhe Gallery, 1932 32.16.5

People never write pretty melodies for tubas. It just isn't
done.

George Kleinsinger and Paul Tripp

Wes Montgomery 1925
American jazz guitarist

Lorin Maazel 1930
American conductor

Dame Kiri Te Kanawa 1944
New Zealand soprano

Maurice Ravel 1875
French composer

Robert Erickson 1917
American composer

The horn, the horn, the lusty horn
Is not a thing to laugh to scorn.

William Shakespeare

Hunting Horn
Glazed earthenware
French, late 18th–early 19th century

The Crosby Brown Collection of Musical Instruments,
1889   89.4.1115

March 8

Carl Philipp Emanuel Bach 1714
German composer

Ruggero Leoncavallo 1857
Italian composer

Alan Hovhaness 1911
American composer

March 9

Samuel Barber 1910
American composer

John Beckwith 1927
Canadian composer and
music critic

Thomas Schippers 1930
American conductor

Ruggero Leoncavallo
Caricature signed "Lindlott," 1913
Pen and ink

The Muller Collection, Music Division
The New York Public Library

I have always believed that I need a circumference of
silence. As to what happens when I compose, I really
haven't the faintest idea.

Samuel Barber

It is clear that the first specification for a composer is to
be dead.

Arthur Honegger

March
10

Pablo de Sarasate 1844
  Spanish violinist

Arthur Honegger 1892
  French composer

"Bix" Beiderbecke 1903
  American jazz cornetist

March
11

Carl Ruggles 1876
  American composer

Henry Dixon Cowell 1897
  American composer

Lawrence Welk 1903
  American accordionist
  and conductor of
  "champagne" music

Enjoying Cherry Blossom Viewing at Ueno (detail)
Yōshū Chikanobu, Japanese, 1838–1912
Polychrome woodblock print, 1887
  Gift of Lincoln Kirstein, 1959   JP3306

March 12

Thomas Arne 1710
English composer

Liza Minnelli 1946
American actress and singer
of popular music

James Taylor 1948
American folk-rock singer,
songwriter, and guitarist

March 13

Hugo Wolf 1860
Austrian composer

Fritz Busch 1890
German conductor

Neil Sedaka 1939
American songwriter and
singer of popular music

March 14

Georg Philipp Telemann 1681
German composer

Johann Strauss, Sr. 1804
Austrian composer; "The
Father of the Waltz"

Quincy Delight Jones, Jr. 1933
American jazz composer,
trumpeter, bandleader, and
pianist

March 15

Harry James 1916
American jazz trumpeter and
bandleader

Cecil Taylor 1933
American jazz pianist and
composer

Sly Stone 1944
American soul-rock singer and
instrumentalist

rauss Performs Today
hograph by Otto Böhler of Johann
rauss, Sr., conducting while fourteen
at composers dance. (See key below
identification of composers.)
strian, late 19th–early 20th century
The Muller Collection, Music Division
The New York Public Library

ere he [Johann Strauss, Sr.] fiddles,
dance–dance they must. . . . He
nself dances, body and soul, while he
ys–not with his feet but with his
lin, which keeps bobbing up and
wn while the whole man marks the
ent of every bar.

Ignaz Moscheles

March 16

Christa Ludwig 1924
German mezzo-soprano

Teresa Berganza 1935
Spanish mezzo-soprano

David Del Tredici 1937
American composer

March 17

Nat "King" Cole 1917
American jazz singer and pianist

Paul Horn 1930
American jazz flutist, saxophonist, clarinetist, and composer

John Sebastian 1944
American pop-rock singer, songwriter, and guitarist

March 18

Nicolai Rimsky-Korsakov 1844
Russian composer

Gian Francesco Malipiero 1882
Italian composer and musicologist

Wilson Pickett 1941
American soul singer and songwriter

Max Reger
Caricature signed "CS"
Lithograph, 20th century

Creation must be completely free. Every fetter one imposes on oneself by taking into account playability or public taste leads to disaster.

Max Reger

Pour Toi! . . .
Plate two from a song series, *Les Vieilles Histoires*
Henri de Toulouse-Lautrec, French, 1864–1901
Lithograph with stencil coloring
Paris: G. Ondet, 1893

March
19

Max Reger 1873
German composer

Dinu Lipatti 1917
Rumanian pianist and composer

Ornette Coleman 1930
American jazz alto saxophonist and composer

March
20

Lauritz Melchior 1890
Danish-born American tenor

Sviatoslav Richter 1915
Russian pianist

Marian McPartland 1920
British jazz pianist

March 21

Johann Sebastian Bach 1685
German composer

Modest Mussorgsky 1839
Russian composer

Arthur Grumiaux 1921
Belgian violinist

March 22

Stephen Sondheim 1930
American composer and
lyricist of musicals

George Benson 1943
American jazz and pop guitarist
and singer

Andrew Lloyd Webber 1948
British composer

Clavicytherium
Wood and various other materials
German (?), mid-18th century
Gift of Helen C. Lanier, 1981   1981.477

March 23

Franz Schreker 1878
Austrian composer and
conductor

Anthony van Hoboken 1887
Dutch music bibliographer;
cataloguer of the works of
Haydn

Régine Crespin 1927
French soprano

March 24

María Felicità Malibran 1808
Spanish contralto

Byron Janis 1928
American pianist

Benjamin Luxon 1937
British baritone

Bach
Sotéro Cosme, Brazilian
Woodcut, ca. 1940
Gift of Sotéro Cosme, 1944   44.28.7

I was obliged to work hard. Whoever is equally
industrious will succeed just as well.

Johann Sebastian Bach

Bach almost persuades me to be a Christian.

Roger Fry

Bach is a colossus of Rhodes, beneath whom all musicians pass and will continue to pass. Mozart is the most
beautiful, Rossini the most brilliant, but Bach is the most
comprehensive: he has said all there is to say.

Charles Gounod

March
25

Arturo Toscanini 1867
Italian conductor

Béla Bartók 1881
Hungarian composer and
pianist

Aretha Franklin 1942
American soul singer

March
27

Vincent d'Indy 1851
French composer and
conductor

Sarah Vaughan 1924
American jazz singer and
pianist

Mstislav Rostropovich 1927
Soviet cellist and conductor

March
26

Pierre Boulez 1925
French composer and
conductor

Diana Ross 1944
American pop and soul singer

Teddy Pendergrass 1950
American soul singer,
songwriter, and drummer

Music's the cordial of a troubled breast,
The softest remedy that grief can find;
The gentle spell that charms our care to rest
And calms the ruffled passions of the mind.
  Music does all our joys refine,
  And gives the relish to our wine.

John Oldham

Woman with a Lute
Johannes Vermeer, Dutch, 1632–1675
Oil on canvas, ca. 1662–65
  Bequest of Collis P. Huntington, 1900   25.110.24

March 28

Rudolf Serkin 1903
Austrian pianist

Robert Ashley 1930
American composer

Samuel Ramey 1942
American bass

March 29

Sir William Walton 1902
British composer

Pearl Bailey 1918
American jazz singer

Richard Rodney Bennett 1936
British composer

March 30

Sergei Vasilenko 1872
Russian composer

Gordon Mumma 1935
American composer of
experimental music

Eric Clapton 1945
British rock guitarist and singer

Rudolf Serkin
Benedict F. Dolbin, Austrian, 1883–1971
Pen, ink, and pencil

The Dolbin Collection, Music Division
The New York Public Library

Serge Diaghilev and Vaslav Nijinsky
Jean Cocteau, French, 1891–1963
Drawing in felt-tipped pen (1961), after a 1913 drawing

Dance Collection, The New York Public Library
Gift of Mrs. Robert D. Graff

Mina'iware Bowl
Composite body, stain- and overglaze-painted
and gilded
Iranian, late 12th–early 13th century

Gift of Mr. and Mrs. A. Wallace Chauncey, 1957   57.61.16

March
31

Franz Joseph Haydn 1732
Austrian composer

Sergei Diaghilev 1872
Russian impresario; founder of
the *Ballets Russes*

Herb Alpert 1935
American trumpeter,
bandleader, and composer

April 1

Ferruccio Busoni 1866
Italian pianist and composer

Sergei Rachmaninoff 1873
Russian-born American
composer and pianist

Alberta Hunter 1895
American blues singer

April 2

Kurt Herbert Adler 1905
Austrian-born American
conductor and opera director

Marvin Gaye 1939
American soul singer and
songwriter

Leon Russell 1941
American rock singer,
songwriter, and instrumentalist

Portrait of Ferruccio Busoni
Eugen Spiro, American, 1874–1972
Lithograph
Gift of Elsa Neumann, 1968   68.697.35

Take it for granted from the beginning that everything is possible on the piano, even when it seems impossible to you, or really is so.
Ferruccio Busoni

On Rachmaninoff's performing:

Even an ordinary broken chord is made to disclose rare beauties; we are reminded of the fairies' hazelnuts in which diamonds were concealed but you could break the shell only if your hands were blessed.
Neville Cardus

Portrait of Rachmaninoff
Emil Fuchs, American, 1866–1929
Etching
Bequest of Estate of Emil Fuchs, 1931   31.28.

April
3

Mario Castelnuovo-Tedesco 1895
Italian-born American
composer

Wayne Newton 1942
American singer of popular
music

Garrick Ohlsson 1948
American pianist

April
4

Hans Richter 1843
German conductor

Pierre Monteux 1875
French conductor

"Muddy" Waters 1915
American blues singer and
guitarist

April
5

Ludwig Spohr 1784
German violinist, composer,
and conductor

Albert Roussel 1869
French composer

Herbert von Karajan 1908
Austrian conductor

The Trapeze Artists (Les Codomas)
Henri Matisse, French, 1869–1954
Color stencil from *Jazz*
Paris: Tériade, 1947

Gift of Lila Acheson Wallace, 1983   1983.1009 (11)

A jazz musician is a juggler who uses harmonies instead of oranges.

Benny Green

April 6

Edison Denisov 1929
Soviet composer

André Previn 1929
German-born American pianist,
composer, and conductor

Merle Haggard 1937
American country-music
singer, fiddler, and guitarist

April 7

Robert Casadesus 1899
French pianist and composer

Billie Holiday 1915
American jazz singer

Ravi Shankar 1920
Indian sitarist and composer

April 8

Sir Adrian Boult 1889
British conductor

Franco Corelli 1921
Italian tenor

Jacques Brel 1929
Belgian-born French singer and
songwriter

April 9

Efrem Zimbalist 1890
Russian-born American
violinist and composer

Paul Robeson 1898
American bass

Antal Dorati 1906
Hungarian-born American
conductor and composer

Jazz is to be played, sweet, soft, plenty rhythm.

"Jelly Roll" Morton

Arrival of the Brass Section
Fred Becker, American, b. 1913
Engraving, ca. 1937
  Gift of WPA–New York City Project, 1943   43.33.93

■no Player
■d Becker, American, b. 1913
■od engraving, ca. 1937
■larris Brisbane Dick Fund, 1940   40.111.72

play it first and tell you what it is
■er.

Miles Davis

■mehow I suspect that if Shakespeare
■re alive today, he might be a jazz fan
■nself.

Duke Ellington

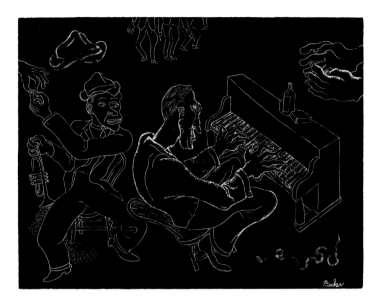

---

pril
12

Lionel Hampton 1913
American jazz vibraphonist,
pianist, drummer, and
bandleader

Montserrat Caballé 1933
Spanish soprano

Herbie Hancock 1940
American jazz pianist and
composer

April
13

Félicien David 1810
French composer

Sir William Sterndale Bennett 1816
British pianist, conductor, and
composer

Margaret Price 1941
British soprano

April
14

Loretta Lynn 1932
American country-music
singer, songwriter, and guitarist

Morton Subotnick 1933
American composer of
experimental music

Julian Lloyd Webber 1951
British cellist

April
16

Henry Mancini 1924
American arranger, composer,
conductor, and pianist

Herbie Mann 1930
American jazz flutist

Dennis Russell Davies 1944
American conductor

April
15

Domenico Gabrieli 1651
Italian composer and cellist

Bessie Smith 1894
American blues, jazz, and
vaudeville singer

Neville Marriner 1924
British violinist and conductor

Music has charms, we all may find,
Ingratiate deeply with the mind.
When art does sound's high power advance,
To music's pipe the passions dance;
Motions unwill'd its powers have shown,
Tarantulated by a tune.

Matthew Green

Dancing in Colombia
Fernando Botero, Colombian, b. 1932
Oil on canvas, 1980
Anonymous Gift, 1983   1983.251

April
17

Artur Schnabel 1882
Austrian-born American
pianist

Gregor Piatigorsky 1903
Russian-born American cellist
and composer

Don Kirshner 1934
American pop-music
entrepreneur

April
18

Franz von Suppé 1819
Austrian composer and
conductor

Leopold Stokowski 1882
British-born American
conductor

Catherine Malfitano 1948
American soprano

April
19

Augustus D. Juilliard 1836
American music patron;
responsible for the founding
of The Juilliard School of Music

Germaine Tailleferre 1892
French composer

Murray Perahia 1947
American pianist and
conductor

April
20

Nicolai Miaskovsky 1881
Russian composer

John Eliot Gardiner 1943
British conductor

Peter Frampton 1950
British rock singer and guitarist

Under the greenwood tree
Who loves to lie with me,
And turn his merry note,
Unto the sweet bird's throat.
Come hither, come hither, come hither:
Here shall he see
No enemy
But winter and rough weather.

William Shakespeare

The God of Music dwelleth out of doors.

Edith M. Thomas

April 21

Estelle Liebling 1880
American soprano

Randall Thompson 1899
American composer

Bruno Maderna 1920
Italian-born German conductor
and composer

Shepherd and Shepherdess
Tapestry of wool and silk
Franco-Netherlandish, late 15th century
Bequest of Susan Vanderpoel Clark, 1967   67.155.8

Yehudi Menuhin
Pencil drawing signed "Tabor," 1929

The Muller Collection, Music Division
The New York Public Library

April
22

Dame Ethel Smyth 1858
British composer

Yehudi Menuhin 1916
American violinist

Charles Mingus 1922
American jazz double-bass
player, pianist, composer,
and bandleader

April
23

Albert Coates 1882
British conductor and
composer

Sergei Prokofiev 1891
Russian composer and pianist

Roy Orbison 1936
American rock-and-roll singer,
songwriter, and guitarist

Improvisation is not the expression of accident but rather
of the accumulated yearnings, dreams, and wisdom of
our very soul.

Yehudi Menuhin

April 24

Giovanni Battista Martini 1706
Italian music scholar and
composer

Violet Archer 1913
Canadian pianist and composer

Barbra Streisand 1942
American actress and singer
of popular music

April 25

Italo Tajo 1915
Italian bass

Ella Fitzgerald 1918
American singer of jazz and
popular music

Albert King 1923
American blues singer and
guitarist

Had I learned to fiddle, I should have done nothing else.

Samuel Johnson

Seated Violinist
Edgar Degas, French, 1834–1917
Black chalk and pastel on green paper, 1877/78
Rogers Fund, 1918   19.51.1

April
26

Gertrude "Ma" Rainey 1886
American blues, jazz, and
vaudeville singer

Joseph Fuchs 1900
American violinist

Bobby Rydell 1942
American rock-and-roll singer
and drummer

April
27

Friedrich von Flotow 1813
German composer

Nicolas Slonimsky 1894
Russian-born American
musicologist, musical
lexicographer, and composer

Judith Blegen 1941
American soprano

April
28

Hermann Suter 1870
Swiss composer and conductor

Louise Homer 1871
American contralto

Nan Merriman 1920
American mezzo-soprano

April
29

Sir Thomas Beecham 1879
British conductor

Duke Ellington 1899
American jazz pianist,
bandleader, and composer

Zubin Mehta 1936
Indian conductor

April 30

Franz Lehár 1870
Austrian composer of operettas

Robert Shaw 1916
American conductor

Willie Nelson 1933
American country-music
singer, songwriter, and guitarist

May 1

Kate Smith 1909
American singer of popular music

Judy Collins 1939
American guitarist, songwriter, and singer
of folk and popular music

Rita Coolidge 1945
American rhythm-and-blues and country-
music singer

The Conductor
Mervin Jules, American, b. 1912
Lithograph, ca. 1945

Museum Acquisition; transferred from the Library,
1962   62.695.44

There are two golden rules for an orchestra:
start together and finish together. The public
doesn't give a damn what goes on in between.

Sir Thomas Beecham

Today, conducting is a question of ego: a lot of
people believe they are actually playing the
music.

Daniel Barenboim

May 2

Alessandro Scarlatti 1660
Italian composer

Lorenz Hart 1895
American lyricist and librettist

Bing Crosby 1901
American actor and singer of popular music

May 3

Richard D'Oyly Carte 1844
British impresario; producer of Gilbert and Sullivan operettas

Pete Seeger 1919
American folk singer, banjo player, guitarist, and songwriter

James Brown 1933
American rhythm-and-blues singer, songwriter, dancer, and instrumentalist

Sir William Gilbert and
Sir Arthur Sullivan
Caricatures signed "L. Binns"
English, late 19th century
Pen and ink

I heard *Rosenkavalier* for the first time after the war and I confess I prefer Gilbert and Sullivan. . . . Sullivan has a sense of timing and punctuation which I have never been able to find in Strauss.

Igor Stravinsky

You ought to write *grand* opera, Sir Arthur, you would do it so well.

Queen Victoria

May 4

Bartolommeo Cristofori 1655
Italian instrument maker; inventor of
the piano

Maynard Ferguson 1928
Canadian jazz trumpeter and bandleader

Roberta Peters 1930
American soprano

May 5

Giulietta Simionato 1910
Italian contralto

Charles Rosen 1927
American pianist, musicologist,
and writer

Tammy Wynette 1942
American country-music singer and
songwriter

May 6

George Perle 1915
American composer and theorist

Godfrey Ridout 1918
Canadian composer

Richard Stilwell 1942
American baritone

May 7

Johannes Brahms 1833
German composer

Piotr Ilyich Tchaikovsky 1840
Russian composer

Elisabeth Söderström 1927
Swedish soprano

Johannes Brahms
Caricature after a pen and ink silhouette by Otto Böhler,
Austrian, late 19th century
Colored paper on paper
Berlin: Werckmeisters Kunstverlag

The Muller Collection, Music Division
The New York Public Library

Johannes Brahms
Two caricatures after pencil sketches by
Willy von Beckerath, German, b. 1868
Lithographs

The Muller Collection, Music Division
The New York Public Library

y things really are written with an appalling lack of acticability!

Johannes Brahms

landscape, torn by mists and clouds, in which I can see ins of old churches, as well as of Greek temples — that Brahms.

Edvard Grieg

once sent him a song and asked him to mark a cross herever he thought it was faulty. Brahms returned it ntouched, saying "I don't want to make a cemetery of ur composition."

Hugo Wolf

May
8

Louis Moreau Gottschalk 1829
American pianist and composer

Mary Lou Williams 1910
American jazz pianist, composer, and arranger

Keith Jarrett 1945
American jazz pianist and composer

May
9

Carlo Maria Giulini 1914
Italian conductor

Hank Snow 1914
Canadian-born American country-music singer, guitarist, and songwriter

Billy Joel 1949
American rock singer, songwriter, and pianist

May 10

Anatoli Liadov 1855
Russian composer

Milton Byron Babbitt 1916
American composer and theorist

Donovan Leitch 1946
Scottish folk singer

May 12

Jules Massenet 1842
French composer

Gabriel Fauré 1845
French composer and organist

Burt Bacharach 1928
American pianist and composer of
popular music

May 11

Joseph "King " Oliver 1885
American jazz cornetist and bandleader

Irving Berlin 1888
Russian-born American songwriter and
lyricist

William Grant Still 1895
American composer

May 13

Sir Arthur Seymour Sullivan 1842
British composer, best known for his
comic operettas

Gil Evans 1912
Canadian jazz pianist, composer, arranger,
and bandleader

Stevie Wonder 1950
American rock singer, songwriter, and
instrumentalist

Otto Klemperer 1885
German conductor

Bobby Darin 1936
American rock-and-roll singer and
songwriter

David Byrne 1952
American rock composer, singer,
performance artist, and movie director

---

les Massenet
aricature signed "SEM"
lor woodcut, 20th century

The Muller Collection, Music Division
The New York Public Library

s very odd! When I hear Massenet's operas I always
ng for Saint-Saëns.' I should add that hearing Saint-
ëns' operas makes me long for Massenet's.

Henri Gauthier-Villars

Relâche
Music by Erik Satie
Sheet-music cover by Francis Picabia,
French, 1879–1953
Color lithograph
Paris: Rouart, Lerolle et Cie., 1926
Music Division, The New York Public Library

Before I compose a piece, I walk round it several times,
accompanied by myself.

Erik Satie

May 15

Claudio Monteverdi 1567
Italian composer

Michael William Balfe 1808
Irish composer

Lars-Erik Larsson 1908
Swedish composer

May 16

Richard Tauber 1891
Austrian-born British tenor

Woody Herman 1913
American jazz clarinetist, bandleader,
and composer

(Walter) Liberace 1919
American pianist and showman

May 17

Erik Satie 1866
French composer

Werner Egk 1901
German composer and conductor

Birgit Nilsson 1918
Swedish soprano

May 18

Ezio Pinza 1892
Italian bass and actor

Meredith Willson 1902
American composer, flutist, arranger,
and orchestrator

Perry Como 1913
American singer of popular music

May 19

Dame Nellie Melba 1861
Australian coloratura soprano

Pete Townshend 1945
British rock guitarist

Grace Jones 1952
Jamaican new-wave singer and songwriter

May 20

Jerzy Fitelberg 1903
Polish composer

Hephzibah Menuhin 1920
American pianist

Joe Cocker 1944
British rock-blues singer and songwriter

You cannot imagine how it spoils one to have been a child prodigy.

Franz Liszt

I know nothing at all about music.

Richard Wagner

Franz Liszt and Richard Wagner
Caricatures of Liszt (above) and Wagner (below)
Pen and ink, ca. 1870

The Muller Collection, Music Division
The New York Public Library

"Fats" Waller 1904
American jazz pianist, organist, singer, bandleader, and composer

Maurice André 1933
French trumpeter

Heinz Holliger 1939
Swiss oboist and composer

Richard Wagner 1813
German composer

Charles Aznavour 1924
French chanteur and composer

John Browning 1933
American pianist

Artie Shaw 1910
American jazz clarinetist, bandleader, composer, and arranger

Alicia de Larrocha 1923
Spanish pianist

Robert A. Moog 1934
American electrical engineer; inventor of the Moog synthesizer

Paul Paray 1886
French conductor and composer

Bob Dylan 1941
American folk and rock singer, songwriter, and guitarist

Patti LaBelle 1944
American soul-rock singer

The Wagnerites
Aubrey Beardsley, British, 1872–1898
Illustration from *The Yellow Book: An Illustrated Quarterly*, Vol. 3, October, 1894
London: John Lane; Boston: Copeland & Day
Thomas J. Watson Library
The Metropolitan Museum of Art

One can't judge Wagner's opera *Lohengrin* after a first hearing, and I certainly don't intend hearing it a second time.

Gioachino Rossini

I have been told that Wagner's music is better than it sounds.

Mark Twain

May 25

Hans Joachim Moser 1889
German musicologist

Miles Davis 1926
American jazz trumpeter, bandleader, and composer

Beverly Sills 1929
American soprano and opera administrator

La Chanteuse Verte
Edgar Degas, French, 1834–1917
Pastel on paper, 1882/85
Bequest of Stephen C. Clark, 1960   61.101.7

There is delight in singing, though none hear
Beside the singer.

Walter Savage Landor

So just, so small, yet in so sweet a note,
It seem'd the music melted in the throat.

John Dryden

May 26

Peggy Lee 1920
American singer of popular music

William Bolcom 1938
American pianist, composer, and writer

Teresa Stratas 1938
Canadian soprano

May 27

Jacques-François-Fromental-Elie Halévy 1799
French composer

Thea Musgrave 1928
Scottish composer

Ramsey Lewis 1935
American jazz pianist, composer, and bandleader

May 28

György Ligeti 1923
Hungarian-born Austrian composer

Dietrich Fischer-Dieskau 1925
German baritone

Gladys Knight 1944
American rhythm-and-blues singer

May 29

Isaac Albéniz 1860
Spanish composer

Erich Wolfgang Korngold 1897
Austrian-born American composer

Iannis Xenakis 1922
Rumanian-born French theorist and composer

May 30

Benny Goodman 1909
American jazz clarinetist, composer, and bandleader

Gustav Leonhardt 1928
Dutch organist and harpsichordist

Olivia Stapp 1940
American soprano

The other arts persuade us, but music takes us by surprise.

Eduard Hanslick

We cannot describe sound, but we cannot forget it either.

Igor Stravinsky

Teukgyeong
Percussion instrument
Marble slab, set in painted wood framework
decorated with ducks, symbolizing joy and fidelity;
phoenixes, symbolizing peace and prosperity; and
pine cones, representing longevity
South Korean, ca. 1981

Gift of Korean Cultural Service, 1982   1982.171.3

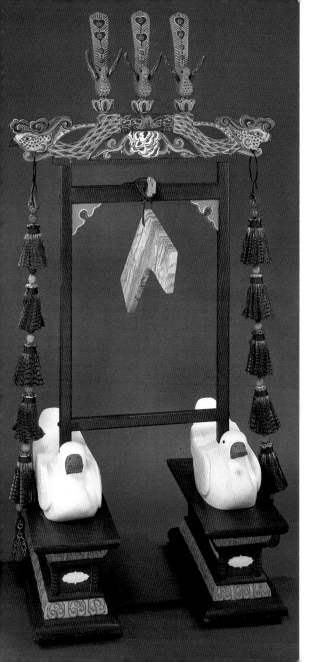

May 31

Alfred Deller 1912
British countertenor

Shirley Verrett 1931
American mezzo-soprano

Peter Yarrow 1938
American folk singer and guitarist

June 1

Mikhail Glinka 1804
Russian composer; "The Father
of Russian Music"

Nelson Riddle 1921
American orchestra leader and
arranger of popular music

Frederica Von Stade 1945
American mezzo-soprano

June 2

Sir Edward Elgar 1857
British composer

Robert Palmer 1915
American composer

Marvin Hamlisch 1944
American pianist, composer,
and arranger of popular music

June 3

Roland Hayes 1887
American tenor

Josephine Baker 1906
American-born French jazz
dancer and singer

Curtis Mayfield 1942
American rhythm-and-blues
singer, songwriter, producer,
and guitarist

Mandolin
Angelo Mannello, Italian-born
American, 1858–1922
Wood, tortoiseshell, ivory, and metal
New York City, ca. 1900
Gift of the family of Angelo Mannello,
1972   1972.111.1

June 4

Erno Rapee 1891
Hungarian conductor

Robert Merrill 1919
American baritone

Gerry Mulligan 1927
American jazz baritone
saxophonist and arranger

June 5

Daniel Pinkham 1923
  American composer

Martha Argerich 1941
  Brazilian pianist

Laurie Anderson 1947
  American composer and
  performance artist

June 6

Aram Khachaturian 1903
  Russian composer

Vincent Persichetti 1915
  American composer

Klaus Tennstedt 1926
  German conductor

Lute Player in a Garden
White satin embroidered in petit point and raised work,
with seed pearls and coral
English, ca. 1650–75
  Rogers Fund, 1929   29.23.1

None knew whether
The voice or the lute was most divine,
So wondrously they went together.

Thomas Moore

June 7

George Szell 1897
Hungarian-born American
conductor

Charles Strouse 1928
American composer of popular
music

Jaime Laredo 1941
Bolivian-born American
violinist

Two Young Girls at the Piano
Pierre Auguste Renoir, French, 1841–1919
Oil on canvas, 1892
Robert Lehman Collection, 1975   1975.1.201

Schumann is the composer of childhood ... both because
he created a children's imaginative world and because
children learn some of their first music in his marvelous
piano albums.

Igor Stravinsky

June 8

Robert Schumann 1810
German composer

"Boz" Scaggs 1944
American rhythm-and-blues
singer and songwriter

Emanuel Ax 1949
Polish-born American pianist

June 9

Carl Nielsen 1865
Danish composer and
conductor

Cole Porter 1891
American composer for the
musical theater

Charles Wuorinen 1938
American composer

June 10

Frederick Loewe 1904
Austrian-born American composer for the musical theater

Judy Garland 1922
American actress and singer of popular music

Bruno Bartoletti 1926
Italian conductor

June 11

Richard Strauss 1864
German composer and conductor

Risë Stevens 1913
American mezzo-soprano

Carlisle Floyd 1926
American opera composer

June 12

Vic Damone 1928
American singer of popular music

Ian Partridge 1938
British tenor

"Chick" Corea 1941
American jazz-rock pianist

June 13

Elisabeth Schumann 1888
German-born American soprano

Carlos Chávez 1899
Mexican composer and conductor

Kurt Equiluz 1929
Austrian tenor

Le Guéridon
Georges Braque, French, 1882–1963
Oil with sand on canvas, 1921–22

Jointly owned by The Metropolitan Museum of Art
and Mrs. Bertram Smith, 1979   1979.481

Music and rhythm find their way into the secret places of
the soul. . . . Musical innovation is full of danger to the
state, for when modes of music change, the laws of the
state always change with them.

Plato

June
15

Edvard Grieg 1843
Norwegian composer

Erroll Garner 1921
American jazz pianist and
composer

Waylon Jennings 1937
American country-music
singer, songwriter, and guitarist

June
16

Otto Jahn 1813
German philologist and
musicographer

Willi Boskovsky 1909
Austrian violinist and
conductor

Sergiu Comissiona 1928
Rumanian-born American
conductor

une
17

Igor Stravinsky 1882
Russian-born American
composer

Mignon Dunn 1932
American mezzo-soprano

Barry Manilow 1946
American singer, composer, and
arranger of popular music

June
18

Charles Gounod 1818
French composer, conductor,
and organist

Paul McCartney 1942
British rock singer, songwriter,
and guitarist

Eva Marton 1948
Hungarian soprano

never understood the need for a "live" audience. My
music, because of its extreme quietude, would be
happiest with a dead one.

Igor Stravinsky

u can rave about Stravinsky without the slightest risk
being classed as a lunatic by the next generation.

George Bernard Shaw

w music? Hell, there's been no new music since
ravinsky.

Duke Ellington

June
19

Johann Wenzel Stamitz 1717
Bohemian violinist, conductor,
and composer

Alfredo Catalani 1854
Italian composer

Guy Lombardo 1902
Canadian-born American
bandleader

June 20

Jacques Offenbach 1819
German-born French conductor, cellist, and composer of operettas

Chet Atkins 1924
American country-music guitarist

André Watts 1946
American pianist

What else is *opéra comique*, in fact, but sung vaudeville?

Jacques Offenbach

. . . I got to try the bagpipes. It was like trying to blow an octopus.

James Galway

Seated Man Playing Bagpipes
Attributed to Pieter Bruegel the Younger, Flemish, 1564–1638
Pen and brown ink
Bequest of Harry G. Sperling, 1971   1975.131.172

June 21

Hilding Rosenberg 1892
Swedish composer

Alois Hába 1893
Czech composer and writer

Judith Raskin 1932
American soprano

June 23

Carl Reinecke 1824
German pianist, composer, and conductor

Mieczyslaw Horszowski 1892
Polish pianist

James Levine 1943
American conductor and pianist

June 22

Jennie Tourel 1900
Russian-born American mezzo-soprano

Sir Peter Pears 1910
British tenor

Kris Kristofferson 1936
American country-rock singer, songwriter, and actor

June 24

Harry Partch 1901
American composer and inventor of musical instruments

Pierre Fournier 1906
French cellist

Terry Riley 1935
American avant-garde composer

June 25

Gustave Charpentier 1860
French composer

Hans Barth 1897
German pianist and composer

Carly Simon 1945
American folk-rock singer and
songwriter

June 26

Giuseppe Taddei 1916
Italian baritone

Jacob Druckman 1928
American composer

Claudio Abbado 1933
Italian conductor

June 27

Mildred Hill 1859
American organist and pianist;
composer of "Happy Birthday
to You"

Karel Reiner 1910
Czech composer and pianist

George Walker 1922
American composer and pianist

June 28

King Henry VIII 1491
English monarch and
occasional composer

Joseph Joachim 1831
Hungarian violinist, composer,
and conductor

Richard Rodgers 1902
American composer for the
musical theater

Abstract Trio
Paul Klee, German, 1879–1940
Watercolor and transferred printing ink
on paper, bordered with gouache and
black ink, 1923

The Berggruen Klee Collection,
1984   1984.315.36

Music is the art of thinking with sounds.

Jules Combarieu

June
29

Nelson Eddy 1901
American baritone and actor

Frank Loesser 1910
American songwriter and composer
of musical comedies

Rafael Kubelík 1914
Czech-born Swiss conductor
and composer

June
30

Lena Horne 1917
American singer of popular
music

"Buddy" Rich 1917
American jazz drummer and
bandleader

Martin Mailman 1932
American composer

Satchmo
Elliot Elisofon, American, 1911–1973
Chromogenic color print, 1954

    Gift of Photography in the Fine Arts, 1959   59.559.24

If it hadn't been for him, there wouldn't have been
none of us. I want to thank Mr. Louis Armstrong
for my livelihood.

                           "Dizzy" Gillespie

July
1

Hans Werner Henze 1926
German composer

July
2

Christoph Willibald Gluck 1714
German composer

Ahmad Jamal 1930
American jazz pianist

Gilbert Kalish 1935
American pianist

July 3

Leoš Janáček 1854
Czech composer, conductor, and collector of Moravian folk songs

George M. Cohan 1878
American songwriter, vaudeville performer, playwright, and producer

Carlos Kleiber 1930
German conductor

July 4

Stephen Foster 1826
American composer of songs

Louis Armstrong 1900
American jazz trumpeter, singer, and bandleader

Mitch Miller 1911
American conductor and oboist

July 5

Paul Ben-Haim 1897
Israeli composer and student of Middle Eastern folk music

George Rochberg 1918
American composer and music editor

Janos Starker 1924
Hungarian-born American cellist

July 6

Elisabeth Lutyens 1906
British composer

Bill Haley 1925
American rock-and-roll singer, songwriter, and guitarist

Vladimir Ashkenazy 1937
Russian-born Icelandic pianist and conductor

Here Comes the Parade
Louis Barlow, American, b. 1908
Wood engraving, ca. 1937
Gift of WPA—New York City Project, 1943   43.33.18

I like to look on the composer's vocation as the old troubadours or bards did. In those days it was no disgrace to a man to be turned on to step in front of an army and inspire the people with a song.

Sir Edward Elgar

July
7

Gustav Mahler 1860
Austrian composer and conductor

Gian Carlo Menotti 1911
Italian composer and conductor

Ringo Starr 1940
British rock drummer and singer

July
8

Percy Aldridge Grainger 1882
Australian-born American pianist and composer

George Antheil 1900
American composer

Louis W. Ballard 1931
American composer

July 9

Ottorino Respighi 1879
Italian composer and
conductor

David Diamond 1915
American composer

David Zinman 1936
American conductor

July 10

Henryk Wieniawski 1835
Polish violinist

Carl Orff 1895
German composer

Arlo Guthrie 1947
American folk singer and
songwriter

July 11

Nicolai Gedda 1925
Swedish tenor

Herbert Blomstedt 1927
American-born Swedish
conductor

Hermann Prey 1929
German baritone

Bugle
Thomas Key, English, d. 1853
Silver gilt, 1811
Rogers Fund, 1975   1975.270

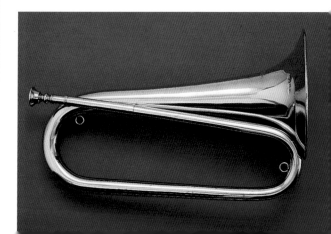

July 12

Kirsten Flagstad 1895
Norwegian soprano

Oscar Hammerstein II 1895
American lyricist for the
musical theater

Van Cliburn 1934
American pianist

Van Cliburn and Leonard Bernstein
René Bouché, French, 1905–1963
Pen and ink
Music Division, The New York Public Library

July 13

Carlo Bergonzi 1924
Italian tenor

Meyer Kupferman 1926
American composer

Per Nørgaard 1932
Danish composer

Any composer's writing is the sum of himself, of all his
roots and influences. I have deep roots, each different
from one another. . . . I can only hope it adds up to
something you could call universal.

Leonard Bernstein

July 14

Gerald Finzi 1901
British composer

Woody Guthrie 1912
American folk singer,
songwriter, and author

Alexander Popov 1927
Bulgarian composer

July 15

Julian Bream 1933
British guitarist and lutenist

Harrison Birtwistle 1934
British composer

Linda Ronstadt 1946
American singer of rock and
popular music

The harmonic effects which our guitarists produce
unconsciously represent one of the marvels of natural art.

Manuel de Falla

The Spanish Singer
Edouard Manet, French, 1832–1883
Oil on canvas, 1860
Gift of William Church Osborn, 1949   49.58.2

Siyavush and Farangis Wedded
Details from a miniature in the *Shah-nameh*
Probably by Qasim, son of 'Ali
Colors, ink, silver, and gold on paper
Iranian, Safavid period, ca. 1525–30

Gift of Arthur A. Houghton, Jr., 1970   1970.301.28
(folio 185v)

July
16

Eugène Ysaÿe 1858
Belgian violinist, conductor,
and composer

Bella Davidovich 1928
Soviet-born American pianist

Pinchas Zukerman 1948
Israeli violinist, violist, and
conductor

July
17

Eleanor Steber 1916
American soprano

Peter Schickele 1935
American composer; creator of
P.D.Q. Bach

Phoebe Snow 1952
American singer of popular
music

July 18

Giovanni Bononcini 1670
Italian composer

Kurt Masur 1927
German conductor

Martha Reeves 1941
American rhythm-and-blues
singer

July 19

Vincenz Lachner 1811
German organist, conductor,
and composer

Klaus Egge 1906
Norwegian composer

Heard melodies are sweet, but those unheard
Are sweeter; therefore, ye soft pipes, play on;
Not to the sensual ear, but, more endeared,
Pipe to the spirit ditties of no tone.

John Keats

July 20

Déodat de Séverac 1872
French composer

Nam June Paik 1932
Korean-born American
avant-garde composer

Carlos Santana 1947
Mexican-born American rock
guitarist

July 21

Isaac Stern 1920
American violinist

Albert Fuller 1926
American harpsichordist

Cat Stevens 1948
British folk-rock singer and
songwriter

July 22

Lucien Fugère 1848
French baritone

Licia Albanese 1913
Italian-born American soprano

Learning music by reading about it is like making love by
mail.

Isaac Stern

Music should either be done in a church or in someone's
home.

Gustav Holst

The Music Room
Mihály de Munkácsy, Hungarian, 1844–1900
Oil on wood

Bequest of Mrs. Martha T. Fiske Collord, in memory of
Josiah M. Fiske, 1908   08.136.11

Don't perspire while conducting—only the audience should get warm.

Richard Strauss

Serge Koussevitzky
Caricature signed "Quiz"
Woodcut, 20th century

The Muller Collection, Music Division
The New York Public Library

Franz Adolf Berwald 1796
Swedish composer and
violinist

Ben Weber 1916
American composer

Leon Fleisher 1928
American pianist and
conductor

Ernest Bloch 1880
Swiss-born American
composer and conductor

Mick Fleetwood 1947
British rock drummer

Peter Serkin 1947
American pianist

Alfredo Casella 1883
Italian composer, pianist,
conductor, and writer

Johnny Hodges 1906
American jazz alto and soprano
saxophonist

Maureen Forrester 1930
Canadian contralto

July
26

Serge Koussevitzky 1874
Russian-born American
conductor, double-bass player,
and music publisher

Alexis Weissenberg 1929
Bulgarian-born French pianist

Mick Jagger 1944
British rock singer and
songwriter

Seated Man with Harp
Marble
Cycladic, 3000–2500 B.C.
  Rogers Fund, 1947   47.100.1

There is geometry in the humming of the strings. There is
music in the spacings of the spheres.

Pythagoras

July 27

Enrique Granados 1867
Spanish composer and conductor

Ernö Dohnányi 1877
Hungarian pianist, composer, and conductor

Leonard Rose 1918
American cellist

July 28

Giulia Grisi 1811
Italian soprano

Peter Duchin 1937
American bandleader

Riccardo Muti 1941
Italian conductor

July 29

Sigmund Romberg 1887
Hungarian-born American composer of operettas

Charlie Christian 1916
American guitarist and blues singer

Peter Schreier 1935
German tenor

July 30

Gerald Moore 1899
British pianist and accompanist

Martin Bookspan 1926
American music critic, administrator, and broadcaster

Paul Anka 1941
Canadian singer and songwriter of popular music

Summer Music
Walter Hatke, American, b. 1948
Oil on canvas, 1980

Gift of Mr. and Mrs. Klaus G. Perls,
1984   1984.260

The painter turns a poem into a
painting; the musician sets a
picture to music.

Robert Schumann

July
31

François Auguste Gevaert 1828
Belgian composer,
musicologist, conductor, and
organist

Jan La Rue 1918
American musicologist

Norman Del Mar 1919
British conductor

August
1

Francis Scott Key 1779
American lawyer; author of the
words of "The Star-Spangled
Banner"

Angela Diller 1877
American pianist and educator

Jerry Garcia 1942
American rock guitarist and
singer

August 2

Sir Arthur Bliss 1891
British composer

Karl Amadeus Hartmann 1905
German composer

August 4

William Howard Schuman 1910
American composer, educator, and music administrator

Gabriella Tucci 1929
Italian soprano

Simon Preston 1938
British organist

August 3

Francisco Asenjo Barbieri 1823
Spanish composer

Louis Gruenberg 1884
Polish-born American composer

Tony Bennett 1926
American singer of popular music

I am never merry when I hear sweet music.

William Shakespeare

Mezzetin
Jean Antoine Watteau, French, 1684–1721
Oil on canvas, 1718–20
Munsey Fund, 1934   34.138

August 5

Leonardo Leo 1694
Italian composer and organist

Ambroise Thomas 1811
French composer, primarily
of operas

Erich Kleiber 1890
Austrian conductor

August 6

Hermann Mendel 1834
German music lexicographer

Karl Ulrich Schnabel 1909
German pianist and composer

The Guitar
Henri Laurens, French, 1885–1954
Painted terra-cotta, 1919
Gift of Mr. and Mrs. Daniel Saidenberg, 1984   1984.209

The sense of music is a primal thing in mankind,
and a tremendous force, either for good or evil.

Sir Arthur Bliss

Fauns and a Goat
Pablo Picasso, Spanish, 1881–1973
Linoleum cut, 1959

The Mr. and Mrs. Charles Kramer Collection, Gift of
Mr. and Mrs. Charles Kramer, 1979   1979.620.30

August
7

Henry Charles Litolff 1818
French pianist, composer, and
music publisher

Karel Husa 1921
Czech-born American
composer and conductor

Rahsaan Roland Kirk 1936
American jazz musician

August
8

André Jolivet 1905
French composer and
conductor

Benny Carter 1907
American jazz alto saxophonist,
trumpeter, composer, and
arranger

Roger Nixon 1921
American composer

August 9

Reynaldo Hahn 1874
Venezuelan-born French composer, conductor, and music critic

Zino Francescatti 1902
French violinist

August 11

Carrie Jacobs Bond 1862
American composer

Ginette Neveu 1919
French violinist

Raymond Leppard 1927
British conductor and harpsichordist

August 10

Alexander Glazunov 1865
Russian composer, conductor, and educator

Douglas Stuart Moore 1893
American composer and educator

Eliot Fisk 1954
American guitarist

August 12

Heinrich Biber 1644
Bohemian violinist and composer

"Buck" Owens 1929
American country-music guitarist and singer

Peter Hofmann 1944
German tenor and rock singer

Opera Costume Design
Colored-paper collage, possibly German,
early 20th century
  Music Division, The New York Public Library.

An opera may be allowed to be extravagantly lavish in its decorations, as its only design is to gratify the senses, and keep up an indolent attention in the audience.

Joseph Addison

On opera:

One of the most magnificent and expenseful diversions the wit of man can invent.

John Evelyn

August
13

Sir George Grove 1820
  British musicographer and
  educator

George Shearing 1919
  British-born American jazz
  pianist and composer

Kathleen Battle 1948
  American soprano

August
14

Leone Sinigaglia 1868
  Italian composer

Brian Fennelly 1937
  American composer, pianist,
  and conductor

David Crosby 1941
  American rock singer, guitarist,
  and songwriter

August 15

Jacques Ibert 1890
French composer and educator

Lukas Foss 1922
German-born American pianist, conductor, and composer

Oscar Peterson 1925
Canadian jazz pianist

August 17

Nicola Porpora 1686
Italian composer

Abram Chasins 1903
American pianist, composer, writer, and educator

John Cheek 1948
American bass-baritone

August 16

Heinrich Marschner 1795
German opera composer

Gabriel Pierné 1863
French composer, conductor, and organist

Bill Evans 1929
American jazz pianist and composer

August 18

Antonio Salieri 1750
Italian composer and conductor

Leo Slezak 1873
Austrian tenor

Howard Swanson 1907
American composer

Piano
Paul Outerbridge, Jr., American, 1896–1959
Platinum print, 1926

The notes I handle no better than many pianists. But the pauses between the notes—ah—that is where the art resides.

Artur Schnabel

August 21

Count Basie 1904
American jazz pianist and
bandleader

Dame Janet Baker 1933
British mezzo-soprano

Kenny Rogers 1939
American country-music singer

August 22

Claude Debussy 1862
French composer

John Lee Hooker 1917
American blues guitarist and
singer

Karlheinz Stockhausen 1928
German composer

La Cantate à Trois Voix
Pierre Brissaud, French, b. 1885
Illustration from *Gazette du Bon Ton: Arts, Modes &
Frivolités*, No. 5, May, 1914
Paris: Librairie Centrale des Beaux-Arts

Thomas J. Watson Library
The Metropolitan Museum of Art

First, rehearse your song by rote,
To each word a warbling note.
Hand in hand, with fairy grace,
Will we sing and bless this place.

William Shakespeare

Quatre à Sept, ou Une Heure de Musique
Pierre Brissaud, French, b. 1885
Illustration from *Gazette du Bon Ton: Arts, Modes & Frivolités*, No. 7, May, 1913
Paris: Librairie Centrale des Beaux-Arts
Thomas J. Watson Library
The Metropolitan Museum of Art

Singing lieder is like putting a piece of music under a microscope.

Dame Janet Baker

August 25

Stefan Wolpe 1902
German-born American
composer

Leonard Bernstein 1918
American conductor, composer,
and pianist

José Van Dam 1940
Belgian bass-baritone

August 27

Eric Coates 1886
British composer and violist

Lester Willis "Prez" Young 1909
American jazz tenor
saxophonist

Barry Conyngham 1944
Australian composer

August 26

Arthur Loesser 1894
American pianist and writer

Humphrey Searle 1915
British composer and writer

Peter Appleyard 1928
British jazz vibraphonist and
drummer

August 28

Karl Böhm 1894
Austrian conductor

Richard Tucker 1913
American tenor

Dinah Washington 1924
American rhythm-and-blues
singer

The Woodshed
Romare Bearden, American, b. 1914
Cut and pasted paper and cloth with pencil on
Masonite, 1969
George A. Hearn Fund, 1970   1970.19

Music is your own experience, your thoughts, your
wisdom. If you don't live it, it won't come out of your
horn.

Charlie Parker

Flute Player
Limestone
Cypro-Egyptian, ca. 570–540 B.C.

The Cesnola Collection, Purchased by subscription,
1874–76   74.51.2517

It is proportion that beautifies everything, this whole
universe consists of it, and music is measured by it.

Orlando Gibbons

Charlie Parker 1920
American jazz alto
saxophonist

Thomas Stewart 1928
American baritone

Michael Jackson 1958
American rock singer

Percy Goetschius 1853
American music teacher and
critic

Regina Resnik 1922
American soprano

Van Morrison 1945
Irish blues-rock singer,
songwriter, and instrumentalist

August

31

Amilcare Ponchielli 1834
Italian composer

Alan Jay Lerner 1918
American lyricist for the
musical theater

Itzhak Perlman 1945
Israeli-born American violinist

September

1

Johann Pachelbel 1653
German composer and organist

Engelbert Humperdinck 1854
German composer

Seiji Ozawa 1935
Japanese conductor

At first I thought I should be a second Beethoven; presently I found that to be another Schubert would be good; then, gradually, satisfied with less and less, I was resigned to be a Humperdinck.

Engelbert Humperdinck

Harp Player
Limestone
Cypro-Egyptian, ca. 570–540 B.C.
The Cesnola Collection, Purchased by subscription,
1874–76   74.51.2509

September 2

Isidor Philipp 1863
French pianist

Friedrich Schorr 1888
Hungarian bass-baritone

David Blake 1936
British composer

September 4

Anton Bruckner 1824
Austrian composer and organist

Darius Milhaud 1892
French composer

Meade "Lux" Lewis 1905
American jazz pianist

September 3

Dorothy Maynor 1910
American soprano and educator

Tom Glazer 1914
American folk singer

Thurston Dart 1921
British musicologist

September 5

Johann Christian Bach 1735
German composer

Giacomo Meyerbeer 1791
German composer

John Cage 1912
American avant-garde composer, pianist, and writer

Still Life – Violin and Music
William Michael Harnett,
American, 1848–1892
Oil on canvas, 1888

Wolfe Fund, Catharine Lorillard
Wolfe Collection, 1963   63.85

The material of music is
sound and silence. Integrating
these is composing.

John Cage

The Love Song (Le Chant d'Amour)
Sir Edward Coley Burne-Jones, British, 1833–1898
Oil on canvas, ca. 1866

The Alfred N. Punnett Endowment Fund, 1947   47.26

Fair Melody! kind Siren! I've no choice;
I must be thy sad servant evermore;
I cannot choose but kneel here and adore.

John Keats

September 6

Vincent Novello 1781
English music publisher, organist, and composer

William Kraft 1923
American percussionist, composer, and conductor

Evgeny Svetlanov 1928
Russian conductor and composer

September 8

Antonin Dvořák 1841
Czech composer

Patsy Cline 1932
American country-music singer

Peter Maxwell Davies 1934
British composer

September 7

Hugh Aitken 1924
American composer

"Sonny" Rollins 1929
American jazz tenor saxophonist

Buddy Holly 1936
American rock-and-roll singer and guitarist

September 9

Girolamo Frescobaldi 1583
Italian organist and composer

Edward Burlingame Hill 1872
American composer

Otis Redding 1941
American rhythm-and-blues singer and songwriter

Niccolò Jommelli 1714
Italian composer

Yma Sumac 1927
Peruvian singer

Christopher Hogwood 1941
British harpsichordist,
musicologist, and conductor

Banquet Scene with Musicians
Detail of a facsimile wall painting from the Tomb of
Nakhte: Egyptian (Thebes), 18th Dynasty, ca. 1425 B.C.
Tempera on paper, ca. 1907/11
Rogers Fund, 1915   15.5.9d

It is the best of trades, to make songs, and the second best
to sing them.

Hillaire Belloc

Troubadour
Katsushika Hokusai, Japanese, 1760–1849
Study from an album of drawings
Ink and color on paper
Charles Stewart Smith Collection, Gift of Mrs. Charles Stewart
Smith, Charles Stewart Smith, Jr. and Howard Caswell Smith,
in memory of Charles Stewart Smith, 1914   14.76.60 (87)

September 11

Friedrich Kuhlau 1786
German-born Danish composer and pianist

Alice Tully 1911
American mezzo-soprano and music patron

Arvo Pärt 1935
Estonian composer

September 13

Clara Schumann 1819
German pianist and composer

Arnold Schoenberg 1874
Austrian-born American composer

Robert Ward 1917
American composer

September 12

Maurice Chevalier 1888
French chanteur and actor

Adolph Weiss 1891
American composer and bassoonist

Booker T. Jones 1944
American rock-and-roll musician

September 14

Michael Haydn 1737
Austrian composer

Luigi Cherubini 1760
Italian composer

Lehman Engel 1910
American composer, conductor, and writer

Cowboy Singing
Thomas Eakins, American, 1844–1916
Watercolor on paper
Fletcher Fund, 1925   25.97.5

The way to write American music is simple. All you have
to do is be an American and then write any kind of music
you wish.

Virgil Thomson

September
15

Bruno Walter 1876
German-born American
conductor

Bobby Short 1926
American pianist and singer of
popular music

Jessye Norman 1945
American soprano

September
16

John Gay 1685
English librettist

Nadia Boulanger 1887
French composition teacher

"B. B." King 1925
American blues singer and
guitarist

September 17

Vincenzo Tommasini 1878
Italian composer

Charles Tomlinson Griffes 1884
American composer

Hank Williams 1923
American country-western
singer and songwriter

September 19

Gustav Schirmer 1829
German music publisher

Blanche Thebom 1918
American mezzo-soprano

Cass Elliot 1941
American folk-pop singer

September 18

Emil Scaria 1838
Austrian bass-baritone

Josef Tal 1910
Polish-born Israeli composer
and pianist

Frankie Avalon 1940
American rock-and-roll singer

September 20

Ildebrando Pizzetti 1880
Italian composer and educator

"Jelly Roll" Morton 1885
American jazz pianist and
composer

Laurie Spiegel 1945
American composer

September 21

Francis Hopkinson 1737
American statesman, composer,
and writer

Gustav Holst 1874
British composer and
conductor

Leonard Cohen 1934
Canadian folk singer,
songwriter, and poet

September 23

John Coltrane 1926
American jazz tenor
saxophonist

Ray Charles 1930
American soul singer, pianist,
and songwriter

Bruce Springsteen 1949
American rock singer and
songwriter

September 22

Henryk Szeryng 1918
Polish-born Mexican violinist

William O. Smith 1926
American composer and jazz
clarinetist

Anna Tomowa-Sintow 1941
Bulgarian soprano

September 24

Cornell MacNeil 1922
American baritone

Alfredo Kraus 1927
Spanish tenor

Pablo Elvira 1938
Puerto Rican baritone

nus and the Lute Player

tian, Italian (Venetian), b. ca. 1488, d. 1576

l on canvas

Munsey Fund, 1936   36.29

He capers nimbly in a lady's chamber
To the lascivious pleasing of a lute.

William Shakespeare

September 25

Jean-Philippe Rameau 1683
French composer, theorist, and organist

Dmitri Shostakovich 1906
Soviet composer

Glenn Gould 1932
Canadian pianist

Design for a Piano Screen
For Northome in Wayzata, Minnesota
Frank Lloyd Wright (American, 1867–1956) and Studio
Pencil and colored pencils on tissue, ca. 1912–14
   Purchase, Emily Crane Chadbourne Bequest, 1972   1972.607.

George Gershwin died last week. I don't have to believe it if I don't want to.

John O'Hara

September 26

George Gershwin 1898
American composer

Fritz Wunderlich 1930
German tenor

Olivia Newton-John 1948
British country-music and rock singer

September 27

Bud Powell 1924
American jazz pianist and composer

Igor Kipnis 1930
American harpsichordist

Misha Dichter 1945
American pianist

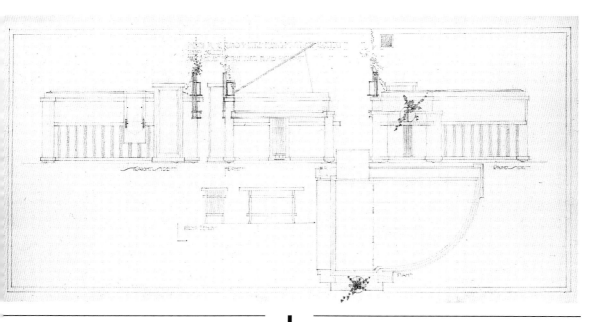

September 30

Sir Charles Villiers Stanford 1852
Irish composer and organist

David Oistrakh 1908
Russian violinist

Johnny Mathis 1935
American singer of popular music

October 2

Henri Février 1875
French composer

Michel Dimitri Calvocoressi 1877
French music writer

Peter Frankl 1935
Hungarian-born British pianist

October 1

Paul Dukas 1865
French composer and music critic

Vladimir Horowitz 1904
Russian-born American pianist

Julie Andrews 1935
British singer and actress

October 3

Steve Reich 1936
American avant-garde composer

Chubby Checker 1941
American rock-and-roll singer

Ruggero Raimondi 1941
Italian bass

October
4

Fanny Persiani 1812
  Italian coloratura soprano

John Aler 1949
  American tenor

October
5

Jürgen Jürgens 1925
  German conductor

Ken Noda 1962
  American pianist and composer

cannot tell you how much I love to play for people. Would you believe it—sometimes when I sit down to practice and there is no one else in the room, I have to stifle an impulse to ring for the elevator man and offer him money to come in and hear me.

Artur Rubinstein

Grand Pianoforte
Marquetry by George Henry Blake
Inlay of wood, ivory, mother-of-pearl,
metal, and various other materials
Erard and Co., English (London),
ca. 1840

Gift of Mrs. Henry McSweeney,
1959   59.76

October 6

Jenny Lind 1820
Swedish coloratura soprano;
"The Swedish Nightingale"

Karol Szymanowski 1882
Polish composer

Paul Badura-Skoda 1927
Austrian pianist and music
editor

October 7

William Billings 1746
American composer

Alfred Wallenstein 1898
American cellist and conductor

Yo-Yo Ma 1955
Chinese-born American cellist

October 8

Heinrich Schütz 1585
German composer

Kurt Redel 1918
German flutist and conductor

Toru Takemitsu 1930
Japanese composer

eople who make music together cannot be enemies, at
east while the music lasts.

Paul Hindemith

he Studio
Winslow Homer, American, 1836–1910
Oil on canvas, 1867
Samuel D. Lee Fund, 1939   39.14

October 9

Giuseppe Verdi 1813
Italian composer

Camille Saint-Saëns 1835
French composer, organist, and conductor

John Lennon 1940
British rock singer, songwriter, and guitarist

October 10

Paul Creston 1906
American composer and organist

Thelonious Monk 1920
American jazz pianist and composer

Ben Vereen 1946
American dancer and singer of popular music

October 11

Albert Stoessel 1894
American conductor and composer

Art Blakey 1919
American jazz drummer

Viktor Tretyakov 1946
Russian violinist

October 12

Arthur Nikisch 1855
Hungarian conductor

Ralph Vaughan Williams 1872
British composer

Luciano Pavarotti 1935
Italian tenor

uciano Pavarotti
rancesco Scavullo, American, b. 1916
elatin-silver print, 1977
Gift of Francesco Scavullo, in memory of John J. McKendry,
1977   1977.581.10

he success of our operas rests most of the time in the
ands of the conductor. This person is as necessary as a
nor or a prima donna.

Giuseppe Verdi

October
13

Art Tatum 1910
American jazz pianist

Paul Simon 1942
American folk-rock singer,
songwriter, and guitarist

Leona Mitchell 1948
American soprano

October
14

Alexander Zemlinsky 1871
Austrian composer and
conductor

Gary Graffman 1928
American pianist

Rafael Puyana 1931
Colombian harpsichordist

October 15

Alexander Dreyschock 1818
Bohemian pianist

Friedrich Nietzsche 1844
German philosopher and
composer

Karl Richter 1926
German organist and conductor

October 17

Giovanni Matteo Mario 1810
Italian tenor

Herbert Howells 1892
British composer

October 16

William Barclay Squire 1855
British musicologist

Bob Weir 1947
American rock guitarist and
singer

October 18

Lotte Lenya 1898
Austrian actress and singer

Shin'ichi Suzuki 1898
Japanese educator and violin
teacher

Wynton Marsalis 1961
American trumpeter

October 19

Karl-Birger Blomdahl 1916
Swedish composer

Emil Gilels 1916
Russian pianist

Benita Valente 1939
American soprano

Woman Playing a Dizi
Detail of a sleeveband from a woman's informal jacket
Satin embroidered in plain and gold-wrapped silks
Chinese, late Ch'ing period, 19th century
Gift of Estate of Tamar Rustow, 1982   1982.466.1

Music is no illusion, but rather a revelation. Its triumphant power lies in the fact that it reveals to us beauties we find in no other sphere; and the apprehension of them is not transitory, but a perpetual reconcilement to life.

Piotr Ilyich Tchaikovsky

October 20

Charles Edward Ives 1874
American composer

Robert Craft 1923
American conductor and writer

Jerry Orbach 1935
American singer and actor for
the musical theater

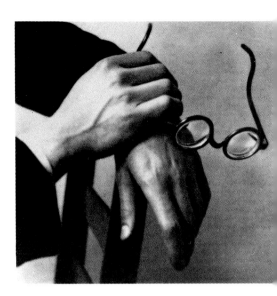

October 21

Egon Wellesz 1885
Austrian composer and
musicologist

Sir Georg Solti 1912
Hungarian-born British
conductor

"Dizzy" Gillespie 1917
American jazz trumpeter and
bandleader

The Hands of Paul Arma
André Kertész, Hungarian-born American, 1894–1985
Gelatin-silver print, 1928
Mr. and Mrs. Noel Levine Gift, and matching funds from the
National Endowment for the Arts, 1979   1979.687

Composition is notation of distortion of what composer
think they've heard before. Masterpieces are marvelou
misquotations.

Ned Rorer

Civilisation . . .
Music by Paul Arma, words by René Maran
Sheet-music cover by Fernand Léger, French, 1881–195
Lithograph
Paris: Heugel et Cie., 1953
Music Division, The New York Public Library

October
22

Franz Liszt 1811
Hungarian composer and pianist

Paul Arma 1904
Hungarian composer and theorist

Paul Zukofsky 1943
American violinist

October
23

Albert Lortzing 1801
German composer

Miriam Gideon 1906
American composer

Ned Rorem 1923
American composer and writer

October
24

"Sonny" Terry 1911
American blues singer and harmonica player

Luciano Berio 1925
Italian composer

George Crumb 1929
American composer and teacher

Paul Arma · René Maran · F. Léger

Civilisation...

October 25

Johann Strauss, Jr. 1825
Austrian composer;
"The Waltz King"

Georges Bizet 1838
French composer

Ransom Wilson 1951
American flutist and conductor

October 26

Domenico Scarlatti 1685
Italian composer and
harpsichordist

Mahalia Jackson 1911
American soul and gospel
singer

Portrait of Paganini
J.A.D. Ingres, French, 1780–1867
Pencil, heightened with white chalk, 1819
Bequest of Grace Rainey Rogers, 1943   43.85.10

Niccolò Paganini 1782
  Italian violinist and composer

Dominick Argento 1927
  American composer

Edda Moser 1941
  German soprano

Everybody is talking about Paganini and his violin. The man seems to be a miracle. The newspapers say that long streamy flakes of music fall from his string, interspersed with luminous points of sound which ascend the air and appear like stars. This eloquence is quite beyond me.

Thomas Macaulay

Paganini
Leon Bakst, French, 1868–1924
Illustration from *Inedited Works of Bakst*
New York: Reau, Roche, Scietlov and Tessier, 1927
  Thomas J. Watson Library
  The Metropolitan Museum of Art

Howard Hanson 1896
  American composer, educator, and conductor

Josef Gingold 1909
  Russian-born American violinist

Charlie Daniels 1936
  American country-music violinist

October
29

Fanny Brice 1891
American singer and comedienne

"Zoot" Sims 1925
American jazz tenor and alto saxophonist and clarinetist

Jon Vickers 1926
Canadian tenor

October
30

Peter Warlock 1894
British composer and writer

Grace Slick 1939
American rock singer and songwriter

Shlomo Mintz 1957
Russian-born Israeli violinist

Girl at the Piano
Édouard Vuillard, French, 1868–1940
Oil on board, ca. 1897
Robert Lehman Collection, 1975   1975.1.224

sit down to the piano regularly at nine o'clock in the morning and *Mesdames les Muses* have learned to be on time for that rendezvous.

Piotr Ilyich Tchaikovsky

If I don't practice for one day, I know it; if I don't practice for two days, the critics know it; if I don't practice for three days, the audience knows it.

Ignacy Jan Paderewski

October
31

Ethel Waters 1896
American blues and jazz singer

Louise Talma 1906
American composer

Tom Paxton 1937
American folk singer, guitarist, and songwriter

November 1

Eugen Jochum 1902
German conductor

Jan Tausinger 1921
Rumanian-born Czech
composer

Victoria de Los Angeles 1923
Spanish soprano

November 3

Samuel Scheidt 1587
German organist and composer

Vincenzo Bellini 1801
Italian composer

Vladimir Ussachevsky 1911
Russian-born American
composer

November 2

Karl Ditters von Dittersdorf 1739
Austrian composer and
violinist

Keith Emerson 1944
British rock keyboardist

Giuseppe Sinopoli 1946
Italian conductor and composer

November 4

Carl Tausig 1841
Polish pianist

Paul Rovsing Olsen 1922
Danish composer,
ethnomusicologist, and
music critic

Anthony Vazzana 1922
American composer

Double Virginal
Hans Ruckers the Elder, Flemish, b. ca. 1540–1550,
d. 1598
Wood and various other materials, 1581
Gift of B. H. Homan, 1929   29.90

Musick is a tonick to the saddened soul, a Roaring Meg against Melancholy, to rear and revive the languishing soul, affecting not only the ears, but the very arteries, the vital and animal spirits; it erects the mind, and makes it nimble.

Robert Burton

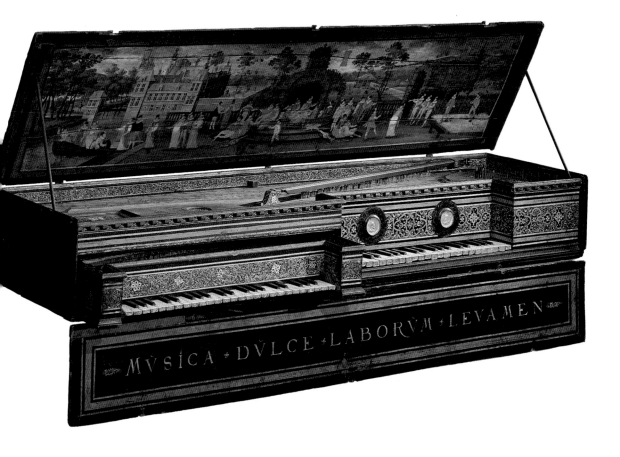

MVSICA · DVLCE · LABORVM · LEVAMEN

November 5

Walter Gieseking 1895
German pianist

Ike Turner 1931
American soul-rock singer,
pianist, and guitarist

Art Garfunkel 1941
American folk-rock singer,
songwriter, and actor

November 6

Adolphe Sax 1814
Belgian instrument maker;
inventor of the saxophone

John Philip Sousa 1854
American bandmaster and
composer; "The March King"

Ray Conniff 1916
American conductor, arranger,
and composer of popular music

The
Bandmaster

The Bandmaster
Caricature of John Philip Sousa signed "Tom B."
Pen and ink, late 19th–early 20th century

The Muller Collection, Music Division
The New York Public Library

Jazz will endure as long as people hear it through their
feet instead of their brains.

John Philip Sousa

On Sousa:

In certain of his strains he struck an incomparably popular and vital note. He said the national thing in a certain
way that no one else ever achieved, and that could be
said only of this nation. . . . Uncle Sam in his striped hat,
goatee, and trousers, out to lick the world, by gum.

Olin Downes

Trio
Hilda Husik, American, active 1930s
Colored carborundum etching
Gift of Pennsylvania WPA, 1943   43.46.116

Chamber music — a conversation between friends.

Catherine Drinker Bowen

November
7

Dame Joan Sutherland 1926
Australian coloratura soprano

Mary Travers 1937
American folk singer

Joni Mitchell 1943
Canadian folk-rock singer, songwriter, and guitarist

November
8

Jerome Hines 1921
American bass

Patti Page 1927
American singer of popular music

Bonnie Raitt 1949
American blues-rock singer and guitarist

November 9

"Mezz" Mezzrow 1899
American jazz clarinetist and saxophonist

Piero Cappuccilli 1929
Italian baritone

Ivan Moravec 1930
Czech pianist

November 11

Ernest Ansermet 1883
Swiss conductor

Mose Allison 1927
American jazz pianist, trumpeter, and singer

Leslie Parnas 1931
American cellist

November 10

Martin Luther 1483
German religious reformer, composer of hymns, and flutist

François Couperin 1668
French composer and organist

Tim Rice 1944
British author and librettist

November 12

Alexander Borodin 1833
Russian composer

Lucia Popp 1939
Czech soprano

Neil Young 1945
Canadian folk-rock singer, songwriter, and guitarist

Idle Hours
Alden Weir, American, 1852–1919
Oil on canvas, 1888
Gift of Several Gentlemen, 1888   88.7

Nothing is more beautiful than a guitar, except, possibly, two.

Frédéric Chopin

Aaron Copland
Arnold Newman, American, b. 1918
Gelatin-silver print, 1959

You may be sitting in a room reading this book. Imagine one note struck upon the piano. Immediately that one note is enough to change the atmosphere of the room – proving that the sound element in music is a powerful and mysterious agent, which it would be foolish to deride or belittle.

Aaron Copland

November
13

Louis Lefébure-Wély 1817
French organist and composer

George Whitefield Chadwick 1854
American composer and conductor

Joonas Kokkonen 1921
Finnish composer

November
14

Johann Nepomuk Hummel 1778
German pianist and composer

Aaron Copland 1900
American composer and conductor

Art Hodes 1904
Russian-born American jazz pianist

Lutes, flutes, and lyres enervate the mind.

Ovid

La Joueuse de Théorbe
George Barbier, French, 1882–1932
Illustration from *Gazette du Bon Ton: Arts, Modes &
Frivolités*, No. 2, February, 1914
Paris: Librairie Centrale des Beaux-Arts

Thomas J. Watson Library
The Metropolitan Museum of Art

LA JOUEUSE DE THÉORBE
Manteau du soir de Paquin

The "Bab" Ballads: Much Sound and Little Sense
Frontispiece
Text and illustrations by Sir William Schwenck Gilbert,
British, 1836–1911
London: John Camden Hotten, 1869
Gift of Sarah Lazarus, 1921   21.36.92

It has been our purpose to produce something that should be innocent but not imbecile.

Sir William Schwenck Gilbert

November 19

Mikhail Ippolitov-Ivanov 1859
Russian composer and
conductor

Tommy Dorsey 1905
American trombonist and
bandleader

Agnes Baltsa 1944
Greek mezzo-soprano

November 20

Ruth Laredo 1937
American pianist

Meredith Monk 1943
American composer, dancer,
choreographer, and singer

Barbara Hendricks 1948
American soprano

November 21

Coleman Hawkins 1904
American jazz tenor
saxophonist

Malcolm Williamson 1931
Australian composer

Livingston Taylor 1951
American folk singer,
songwriter, and guitarist

November 22

Hoagy Carmichael 1899
American jazz pianist and
songwriter

Lord Benjamin Britten 1913
British composer

Gunther Schuller 1925
American composer, conductor,
French-horn player, and
educator

The soft complaining flute
In dying notes discovers
The woes of hopeless lovers,
Whose dirge is whisper'd by the warbling lute.

John Dryden

The Music Lesson
John George Brown, American, 1831–1913
Oil on canvas, 1870
Gift of Colonel Charles A. Fowler, 1921   21.115.3

November 23

Manuel de Falla 1876
Spanish composer and
conductor

Jerry Bock 1928
American songwriter for the
musical theater

Krzysztof Penderecki 1933
Polish composer

November 24

Lilli Lehmann 1848
German soprano

Scott Joplin 1868
American ragtime composer
and pianist

Alfred Schnittke 1934
Soviet composer

November 25

Giuseppe Guarneri 1666
Italian violin maker

Virgil Thomson 1896
American composer, conductor,
and music critic

Paul Desmond 1924
American jazz alto saxophonist
and composer

November 27

Sir Julius Benedict 1804
German-born English
conductor and composer

Charles Koechlin 1867
French composer

Jimi Hendrix 1942
American rock guitarist, singer,
and songwriter

November 26

Eugene Istomin 1925
American pianist

Alan Stout 1932
American composer

Tina Turner 1938
American soul-rock singer

November 28

Jean-Baptiste Lully 1632
Italian-born French composer

Anton Rubinstein 1829
Russian composer and pianist

Randy Newman 1943
American pop-rock songwriter,
singer, and pianist

Lira da Braccio and Portative Organ
Wall detail of the study of Federigo da Montrefeltro,
Duke of Urbino
From the Ducal Palace, Gubbio
Possibly designed by Francesco di Giorgio, Italian
(Sienese, 1439–1502) and others
Executed ca. 1476–80 by Baccio Pontelli of Florence,
with assistants
Walnut, beech, rosewood, oak, and fruitwoods inlaid on
a base of walnut
   Rogers Fund, 1939   39.153

I call architecture frozen music.

Johann Wolfgang von Goethe

November
29

Gaetano Donizetti 1797
Italian composer

Billy Strayhorn 1915
American jazz composer,
lyricist, and pianist

Chuck Mangione 1940
American jazz musician and
composer

November
30

"Brownie" McGhee 1915
American jazz singer and
guitarist

Paul Stookey 1937
American folk singer, songwriter
and guitarist

Radu Lupu 1945
Rumanian pianist

December 1

Mary Martin 1913
American singer and actress, primarily for the musical theater

Lou Rawls 1936
American singer of popular music

Bette Midler 1945
American pop-rock singer and actress

December 3

Nicola Amati 1596
Italian violin maker; teacher of Guarneri and Stradivari

Anton Webern 1883
Austrian composer and conductor

Maria Callas 1923
American soprano

December 2

Robert Kajanus 1856
Finnish conductor and composer

Sir John Barbirolli 1899
British conductor and cellist

Jörg Demus 1928
Austrian pianist

Anton Webern
Egon Schiele,
Austrian, 1890–1918
Charcoal, 1917
Music Division,
The New York Public
Library

Your ears will always lead you right, but you must know why.

Anton Webern

December 4

André Campra 1660
French composer

Yvonne Minton 1938
Australian mezzo-soprano

Dennis Wilson 1944
American rock-and-roll singer
and drummer

December 6

Ira Gershwin 1896
American librettist and lyricist

Dave Brubeck 1920
American jazz pianist and
composer

Nikolaus Harnoncourt 1929
German conductor, cellist, and
musicologist

December 5

Francesco Geminiani 1687
Italian violinist, writer, and
composer

José Carreras 1946
Spanish tenor

Jim Messina 1947
American rock guitarist and
singer

December 7

Pietro Mascagni 1863
Italian composer and conductor

Ernst Toch 1887
Austrian-born American
composer

Harry Chapin 1942
American folk-rock singer and
songwriter

Youthful Musicians with Wind Instruments
Pomponio Amalteo, Italian, 1505–1588
Design for a pendentive
Pen and brown ink, brown wash, heightened with white,
over red chalk, on blue paper
Harry G. Sperling Fund, 1977   1977.249c

Sibelius justified the austerity of his old age by saying
that while other composers were engaged in manufactur-
ing cocktails he offered the public pure cold water.

Neville Cardus

December
8

Jean Sibelius 1865
Finnish composer

Sammy Davis, Jr. 1925
American singer of popular
music

James Galway 1939
Irish flutist

December
9

Elisabeth Schwarzkopf 1915
German soprano

Tatiana Troyanos 1938
American mezzo-soprano

Joan Armatrading 1950
British rock singer and
songwriter

December 10

César Franck 1822
Belgian composer and organist

Olivier Messiaen 1908
French composer

Morton Gould 1913
American composer, conductor, and pianist

December 11

Hector Berlioz 1803
French composer, conductor, and music critic

Elliot Cook Carter, Jr. 1908
American composer

Brenda Lee 1944
American singer of popular music

December 12

Frank Sinatra 1915
American actor and singer of popular music

Dionne Warwick 1941
American singer of popular music

Grover Washington, Jr. 1943
American jazz saxophonist

December 13

Johann Andreas Streicher 1761
German piano maker

Josef Lhévinne 1874
Russian pianist

Carlos Montoya 1903
Spanish flamenco guitarist

Marcia Jan Kimes, 1940
Norwegian and
friend of Sil Kadis xo x

The Musicians
Caravaggio, Italian (Lombard), 1571–1610
Oil on canvas, 1588
  Rogers Fund, 1952   52.81

Music, as long as it exists, will always take its departure
from the major triad and return to it. The musician cannot
escape it any more than the painter his primary colors or
the architect his three dimensions.

Paul Hindemith

December 14

"Spike" Jones 1911
American bandleader of satiric music

Rosalyn Tureck 1914
American pianist and harpsichordist

Christopher Parkening 1947
American guitarist

Jamie Glenn

December 15

John Hammond 1910
American jazz critic

Alan Freed 1922
American disc jockey

Dave Clark 1942
British rock drummer and singer

December 16

Ludwig van Beethoven 1770
German composer

Zoltán Kodály 1882
Hungarian composer and collector of folk songs

Sir Noel Coward 1899
British composer of musical comedies, actor, and producer

December 17

Domenico Cimarosa 1749
Italian composer

Arthur Fiedler 1894
American violinist and conductor

Paul Butterfield 1942
American blues singer and harmonica player

Tribute to Beethoven
Victor Eckhardt, German, b. 1864
Etching showing the building in Vienna where
Beethoven died, Beethoven's death mask, and an excerpt
from the "Funeral March" of the *Eroica* Symphony

The Muller Collection, Music Division
The New York Public Library

December

18

Edward MacDowell 1860
American composer and pianist

Anita O'Day 1919
American jazz singer

Keith Richards 1943
British rock guitarist and singer

Music is a higher revelation than all wisdom and philosophy, it is the wine of a new procreation, and I am Bacchus who presses out this glorious wine for men and makes them drunk with the spirit.

Ludwig van Beethoven

On his deathbed:

Strange, I feel as if up to now I had written no more than a few notes.

Ludwig van Beethoven

Life can't be all bad when for ten dollars you can buy all the Beethoven sonatas and listen to them for ten years.

William F. Buckley, Jr.

December 19

Fritz Reiner 1888
Hungarian-born American conductor

Edith Piaf 1915
French chanteuse and songwriter

Phil Ochs 1940
American folk singer, songwriter, and guitarist

December 20

Henry Hadley 1871
American composer and conductor

Vagn Holmboe 1909
Danish composer and music critic

John Harbison 1938
American composer and conductor

December 21

Frank Zappa 1940
American rock guitarist, composer, arranger, and songwriter

Michael Tilson Thomas 1944
American conductor and pianist

Andras Schiff 1953
Hungarian pianist

December 22

Edgar Varèse 1883
French-born American composer

Deems Taylor 1885
American composer and writer

André Kostelanetz 1901
Russian-born American conductor and arranger

Do you know that our soul is composed of harmony?

Leonardo da Vinci

Angel
Figure from a carved oak choir stall
French, second half 15th century
Gift of J. Pierpont Morgan, 1917   17.190.378

December
23

Giacomo Puccini 1858
Italian composer

Chet Baker 1929
American jazz trumpeter and
singer

Claudio Scimone 1934
Italian conductor and
musicologist

December
24

Peter Cornelius 1824
German composer and writer

Lucrezia Bori 1887
Spanish lyric soprano

Zara Nelsova 1918
Canadian-born American cellist

December 25

Cab Calloway 1907
American jazz singer and bandleader

Little Richard 1932
American rock-and-roll singer, pianist, and songwriter

Orlando Gibbons 1853
English composer and organist

Music is well said to be the speech of angels.

Thomas Carlyle

Musical Angels
Details from a painting, *Virgin and Child with Four Angels*
Gerard David, Flemish, active by 1484, d. 1523
Oil on wood

December
26

Earle Brown 1926
American avant-garde
composer

Adriana Maliponte 1942
Italian soprano

André-Michel Schub 1952
French-born American pianist

December
27

"Bunk" Johnson 1879
American jazz trumpeter

Oscar Levant 1906
American pianist, composer,
writer, and radio personality

December 28

Roger Sessions 1896
American composer

Earl "Fatha" Hines 1905
American jazz pianist and
bandleader

Edgar Winter 1946
American rock vocalist,
saxophonist, guitarist, and
keyboardist

December 29

Pablo Casals 1876
Spanish cellist and conductor

Peggy Glanville-Hicks 1912
Australian composer and music
critic

December 30

Dmitri Kabalevsky 1904
Russian composer, pianist, and
conductor

Paul Frederic Bowles 1910
American composer and
novelist

Sir David Willcocks 1919
British organist, conductor, and
educator

December 31

Nathan Milstein 1904
Russian-born American
violinist and composer

Odetta 1930
American folk-blues singer and
guitarist

John Denver 1943
American singer and
songwriter of popular music

A MUSICAL FAMILY.

A Musical Family
Thomas Rowlandson, British, 1757–1827
Hand-colored etching
London: R. Ackermann, 1802

The Elisha Whittelsey Collection, The Elisha Whittelsey Fund,
1959   59.533.841

Said Oscar Wilde: "Each man kills the thing he loves."
For example, the amateur musician.

H. L. Mencken

INDEX

Glazunov, Alexander — Aug. 10
Glière, Reinhold — Jan. 11
Glinka, Mikhail — June 1
Gluck, Christoph — July 2
Goetschius, Percy — Aug. 30
Goodman, Benny — May 30
Gordon, Dexter — Feb. 27
Gossec, François-
   Joseph — Jan. 17
Gottschalk, Louis
   Moreau — May 8
Gould, Glenn — Sept. 25
Gould, Morton — Dec. 10
Gounod, Charles — June 18
Graffman, Gary — Oct. 14
Grainger, Percy
   Aldridge — July 8
Granados, Enrique — July 27
Grappelli, Stéphane — Jan. 26
Grieg, Edvard — June 15
Griffes, Charles
   Tomlinson — Sept. 17
Grisi, Giulia — July 28
Grout, Donald Jay — Sept. 28
Grove, Sir George — Aug. 13
Gruenberg, Louis — Aug. 3
Grumiaux, Arthur — March 21
Guarneri, Giuseppe — Nov. 25
Guarneri, Pietro
   Giovanni — Feb. 18
Guthrie, Arlo — July 10
Guthrie, Woody — July 14
Gutiérrez Heras,
   Joaquín — Sept. 28

Hába, Alois — June 21
Hadley, Henry — Dec. 20
Haggard, Merle — April 6
Hahn, Reynaldo — Aug. 9
Haitink, Bernard — March 4
Halévy, Jacques-
   François-Fromental-
   Elie — May 27
Haley, Bill — July 6
Hallé, Sir Charles — April 11

Hamlisch, Marvin — June 2
Hammerstein, Oscar, II — July 12
Hammond, John — Dec. 15
Hampton, Lionel — April 12
Hancock, Herbie — April 12
Handel, George
   Frideric — Feb. 23
Handy, W. C. — Nov. 16
Hanson, Howard — Oct. 28
Harbison, John — Dec. 20
Harnoncourt, Nikolaus — Dec. 6
Harrell, Lynn — Jan. 30
Harris, Roy — Feb. 12
Harrison, George — Feb. 25
Hart, Lorenz — May 2
Hartmann, Karl
   Amadeus — Aug. 2
Havens, Richie — Jan. 21
Hawkins, Coleman — Nov. 21
Haydn, Franz Joseph — March 31
Haydn, Michael — Sept. 14
Hayes, Isaac — Aug. 20
Hayes, Roland — June 3
Heifetz, Jascha — Feb. 2
Hendricks, Barbara — Nov. 20
Hendrix, Jimi — Nov. 27
Henry VIII, King — June 28
Henschel, Sir George — Feb. 18
Henze, Hans Werner — July 1
Herbert, Victor — Feb. 1
Herman, Woody — May 16
Hérold, Ferdinand — Jan. 28
Hess, Dame Myra — Feb. 25
Hill, Edward
   Burlingame — Sept. 9
Hill, Mildred — June 27
Hindemith, Paul — Nov. 16
Hines, Earl "Fatha" — Dec. 28
Hines, Jerome — Nov. 8
Hoboken, Anthony van — March 23
Hodes, Art — Nov. 14
Hodges, Johnny — July 25
Hofmann, Heinrich — Jan. 13
Hofmann, Peter — Aug. 12
Hogwood, Christopher — Sept. 10

Holiday, Billie — April 7
Holliger, Heinz — May 21
Holly, Buddy — Sept. 7
Holmboe, Vagn — Dec. 20
Holst, Gustav — Sept. 21
Homer, Louise — April 28
Honegger, Arthur — March 10
Hooker, John Lee — Aug. 22
Hopkinson, Francis — Sept. 21
Horn, Paul — March 17
Horne, Lena — June 30
Horne, Marilyn — Jan. 16
Horowitz, Vladimir — Oct. 1
Horszowski,
   Mieczyslaw — June 23
Hovhaness, Alan — March 8
Howells, Herbert — Oct. 17
Hummel, Johann
   Nepomuk — Nov. 14
Humperdinck,
   Engelbert — Sept. 1
Hunter, Alberta — April 1
Husa, Karel — Aug. 7

Ibert, Jacques — Aug. 15
Indy, Vincent d' — March 27
Ippolitov-Ivanov,
   Mikhail — Nov. 19
Istomin, Eugene — Nov. 26
Ives, Burl — June 14
Ives, Charles Edward — Oct. 20

Jackson, Mahalia — Oct. 26
Jackson, Michael — Aug. 29
Jackson, Milt "Bags" — Jan. 1
Jagger, Mick — July 26
Jahn, Otto — June 16
Jamal, Ahmad — July 2
James, Harry — March 15
Janáček, Leoš — July 3
Janis, Byron — March 24
Jarrett, Keith — May 8
Jennings, Waylon — June 15
Joachim, Joseph — June 28
Jochum, Eugen — Nov. 1

Name	Date	Name	Date	Name	Date
Joel, Billy	May 9	Krenek, Ernst	Aug. 23	Lipatti, Dinu	March 19
Johnson, "Bunk"	Dec. 27	Kristofferson, Kris	June 22	Liszt, Franz	Oct. 22
Jolivet, André	Aug. 8	Krupa, Gene	Jan. 15	Litolff, Henry Charles	Aug. 7
Jommelli, Niccolò	Sept. 10	Kubelík, Rafael	June 29	Little Richard	Dec. 25
Jones, Booker T.	Sept. 12	Kuhlau, Friedrich	Sept. 11	Lloyd Webber, Andrew	March 22
Jones, Grace	May 19	Kupferman, Meyer	July 13	Lloyd Webber, Julian	April 14
Jones, Quincy				Loeffler, Charles	
Delight, Jr.	March 14	LaBelle, Patti	May 24	Martin	Jan. 30
Jones, "Spike"	Dec. 14	Lachner, Vincenz	July 19	Loesser, Arthur	Aug. 26
Joplin, Janis	Jan. 19	Lalo, Edouard	Jan. 27	Loesser, Frank	June 29
Joplin, Scott	Nov. 24	Lambert, Constant	Aug. 23	Loewe, Frederick	June 10
Juilliard, Augustus D.	April 19	Laredo, Jaime	June 7	Loggins, Kenny	Jan. 7
Jürgens, Jürgen	Oct. 5	Laredo, Ruth	Nov. 20	Lombardo, Guy	June 19
		Larrocha, Alicia de	May 23	Lortzing, Albert	Oct. 23
Kabalevsky, Dmitri	Dec. 30	Larsson, Lars-Erik	May 15	Ludwig, Christa	March 16
Kajanus, Robert	Dec. 2	La Rue, Jan	July 31	Lully, Jean-Baptiste	Nov. 28
Kalish, Gilbert	July 2	Ledbetter, Huddie		Lupu, Radu	Nov. 30
Karajan, Herbert von	April 5	"Leadbelly"	Jan. 21	Luther, Martin	Nov. 10
Kenton, Stan	Feb. 19	Lee, Brenda	Dec. 11	Lutoslawski, Witold	Jan. 25
Kern, Jerome	Jan. 27	Lee, Peggy	May 26	Lutyens, Elisabeth	July 6
Key, Francis Scott	Aug. 1	Leedy, Douglas	March 3	Luxon, Benjamin	March 24
Khachaturian, Aram	June 6	Lefébure-Wély, Louis	Nov. 13	Lynn, Loretta	April 14
King, Albert	April 25	Lehár, Franz	April 30		
King, "B. B."	Sept. 16	Lehmann, Lilli	Nov. 24	Ma, Yo-Yo	Oct. 7
King, Carole	Feb. 9	Leinsdorf, Erich	Feb. 4	Maazel, Lorin	March 6
Kipnis, Igor	Sept. 27	Leitch, Donovan	May 10	MacDowell, Edward	Dec. 18
Kirchner, Leon	Jan. 24	Lennon, John	Oct. 9	Mackerras, Sir Charles	Nov. 17
Kirk, Rahsaan Roland	Aug. 7	Lenya, Lotte	Oct. 18	MacNeil, Cornell	Sept. 24
Kirshner, Don	April 17	Leo, Leonardo	Aug. 5	Maderna, Bruno	April 21
Kitt, Eartha	Jan. 26	Leoncavallo, Ruggero	March 8	Mahler, Gustav	July 7
Kleiber, Carlos	July 3	Leonhardt, Gustav	May 30	Mailman, Martin	June 30
Kleiber, Erich	Aug. 5	Leppard, Raymond	Aug. 11	Malfitano, Catherine	April 18
Klemperer, Otto	May 14	Lerner, Alan Jay	Aug. 31	Malibran, María	
Knight, Gladys	May 28	Levant, Oscar	Dec. 27	Felicità	March 24
Köchel, Ludwig von	Jan. 14	Levine, James	June 23	Malipiero, Gian	
Kodály, Zoltán	Dec. 16	Lewis, Jerry Lee	Sept. 29	Francesco	March 18
Koechlin, Charles	Nov. 27	Lewis, Meade "Lux"	Sept. 4	Maliponte, Adriana	Dec. 26
Kokkonen, Joonas	Nov. 13	Lewis, Ramsey	May 27	Mancini, Henry	April 16
Korngold, Erich		Lhévinne, Josef	Dec. 13	Mangione, Chuck	Nov. 29
Wolfgang	May 29	Liadov, Anatoli	May 10	Manilow, Barry	June 17
Kostelanetz, André	Dec. 22	Liberace, (Walter)	May 16	Mann, Herbie	April 16
Koussevitzky, Serge	July 26	Liebling, Estelle	April 21	Mannes, David	Feb. 16
Kraft, William	Sept. 6	Ligeti, György	May 28	Mario, Giovanni	
Kraus, Alfredo	Sept. 24	Lightfoot, Gordon	Nov. 17	Matteo	Oct. 17
Kreisler, Fritz	Feb. 2	Lind, Jenny	Oct. 6	Marley, Bob	Feb. 5

Marriner, Neville	April 15
Marsalis, Wynton	Oct. 18
Marschner, Heinrich	Aug. 16
Martin, Mary	Dec. 1
Martini, Giovanni Battista	April 24
Marton, Eva	June 18
Mascagni, Pietro	Dec. 7
Massenet, Jules	May 12
Masur, Kurt	July 18
Mathis, Edith	Feb. 11
Mathis, Johnny	Sept. 30
Mayfield, Curtis	June 3
Maynor, Dorothy	Sept. 3
McCartney, Paul	June 18
McGhee, "Brownie"	Nov. 30
McPartland, Marian	March 20
McShann, Jay	Jan. 12
Mehta, Zubin	April 29
Melba, Dame Nellie	May 19
Melchior, Lauritz	March 20
Mendel, Hermann	Aug. 6
Mendelssohn, Felix	Feb. 3
Mendes, Sergio	Feb. 11
Menotti, Gian Carlo	July 7
Menuhin, Hephzibah	May 20
Menuhin, Yehudi	April 22
Mercer, Mabel	Feb. 3
Merman, Ethel	Jan. 16
Merrill, Robert	June 4
Merriman, Nan	April 28
Messiaen, Olivier	Dec. 10
Messina, Jim	Dec. 5
Meyerbeer, Giacomo	Sept. 5
Mezzrow, "Mezz"	Nov. 9
Miaskovsky, Nicolai	April 20
Midler, Bette	Dec. 1
Milhaud, Darius	Sept. 4
Miller, Glenn	March 1
Miller, Mitch	July 4
Miller, Roger	Jan. 2
Milnes, Sherrill	Jan. 10
Milstein, Nathan	Dec. 31
Mingus, Charles	April 22
Minnelli, Liza	March 12

Minton, Yvonne	Dec. 4
Mintz, Shlomo	Oct. 30
Mitchell, Joni	Nov. 7
Mitchell, Leona	Oct. 13
Moll, Kurt	April 11
Monk, Meredith	Nov. 20
Monk, Thelonious	Oct. 10
Monteux, Pierre	April 4
Monteverdi, Claudio	May 15
Montgomery, Wes	March 6
Montoya, Carlos	Dec. 13
Moog, Robert A.	May 23
Moore, Douglas Stuart	Aug. 10
Moore, Gerald	July 30
Moravec, Ivan	Nov. 9
Morrison, Van	Aug. 30
Morton, "Jelly Roll"	Sept. 20
Moser, Edda	Oct. 27
Moser, Hans Joachim	May 25
Moszkowski, Moritz	Aug. 23
Mottl, Felix	Aug. 24
Mozart, Wolfgang Amadeus	Jan. 27
Mulligan, Gerry	June 4
Mumma, Gordon	March 30
Musgrave, Thea	May 27
Mussorgsky, Modest	March 21
Muti, Riccardo	July 28
Nash, Johnny	Aug. 19
Nelson, Willie	April 30
Nelsova, Zara	Dec. 24
Neveu, Ginette	Aug. 11
Newman, Randy	Nov. 28
Newton, Wayne	April 3
Newton-John, Olivia	Sept. 26
Nielsen, Carl	June 9
Nietzsche, Friedrich	Oct. 15
Nikisch, Arthur	Oct. 12
Nilsson, Birgit	May 17
Nixon, Roger	Aug. 8
Noda, Ken	Oct. 5
Nono, Luigi	Jan. 29
Nørgaard, Per	July 13
Norman, Jessye	Sept. 15

Novello, Vincent	Sept. 6
Ochs, Phil	Dec. 19
O'Day, Anita	Dec. 18
Odetta	Dec. 31
Offenbach, Jacques	June 20
Ohlsson, Garrick	April 3
Oistrakh, David	Sept. 30
Oliver, Joseph "King"	May 11
Olsen, Paul Rovsing	Nov. 4
Ono, Yoko	Feb. 18
Orbach, Jerry	Oct. 20
Orbison, Roy	April 23
Orff, Carl	July 10
Ormandy, Eugene	Nov. 18
Owens, "Buck"	Aug. 12
Ozawa, Seiji	Sept. 1
Pachelbel, Johann	Sept. 1
Paganini, Niccolò	Oct. 27
Page, Patti	Nov. 8
Paik, Nam June	July 20
Palmer, Robert	June 2
Paray, Paul	May 24
Parkening, Christopher	Dec. 14
Parker, Charlie	Aug. 29
Parnas, Leslie	Nov. 11
Pärt, Arvo	Sept. 11
Partch, Harry	June 24
Parton, Dolly	Jan. 19
Partridge, Ian	June 12
Pavarotti, Luciano	Oct. 12
Paxton, Tom	Oct. 31
Pears, Sir Peter	June 22
Penderecki, Krzysztof	Nov. 23
Pendergrass, Teddy	March 26
Perahia, Murray	April 19
Pergolesi, Giovanni Battista	Jan. 4
Peri, Jacopo	Aug. 20
Perle, George	May 6
Perlman, Itzhak	Aug. 31
Persiani, Fanny	Oct. 4
Persichetti, Vincent	June 6

Name	Date
Peters, Roberta	May 4
Peterson, Oscar	Aug. 15
Philipp, Isidor	Sept. 2
Piaf, Edith	Dec. 19
Piatigorsky, Gregor	April 17
Pickett, Wilson	March 18
Pierné, Gabriel	Aug. 16
Pinkham, Daniel	June 5
Pinza, Ezio	May 18
Piston, Walter	Jan. 20
Pizzetti, Ildebrando	Sept. 20
Plant, Robert	Aug. 20
Pollini, Maurizio	Jan. 5
Ponchielli, Amilcare	Aug. 31
Ponselle, Rosa	Jan. 22
Ponty, Jean-Luc	Sept. 29
Popov, Alexander	July 14
Popp, Lucia	Nov. 12
Porpora, Nicola	Aug. 17
Porter, Cole	June 9
Poulenc, Francis	Jan. 7
Powell, Bud	Sept. 27
Powell, Laurence	Jan. 13
Powell, Mel	Feb. 12
Praetorius, Michael	Feb. 15
Presley, Elvis	Jan. 8
Preston, Simon	Aug. 4
Previn, André	April 6
Prey, Hermann	July 11
Price, Leontyne	Feb. 10
Price, Margaret	April 13
Pritchard, Sir John	Feb. 5
Prokofiev, Sergei	April 23
Puccini, Giacomo	Dec. 23
Puyana, Rafael	Oct. 14
Queler, Eve	Jan. 1
Quilico, Louis	Jan. 14
Quivar, Florence	March 3
Rachmaninoff, Sergei	April 1
Raimondi, Ruggero	Oct. 3
Rainey, Gertrude "Ma"	April 26
Raitt, Bonnie	Nov. 8
Rameau, Jean-Philippe	Sept. 25
Ramey, Samuel	March 28
Rampal, Jean-Pierre	Jan. 7
Rapee, Erno	June 4
Raskin, Judith	June 21
Ravel, Maurice	March 7
Rawls, Lou	Dec. 1
Redding, Otis	Sept. 9
Redel, Kurt	Oct. 8
Reeves, Martha	July 18
Reger, Max	March 19
Reich, Steve	Oct. 3
Reinecke, Carl	June 23
Reiner, Fritz	Dec. 19
Reiner, Karel	June 27
Resnik, Regina	Aug. 30
Respighi, Ottorino	July 9
Ricciarelli, Katia	Jan. 16
Rice, Tim	Nov. 10
Rich, "Buddy"	June 30
Richards, Keith	Dec. 18
Richter, Hans	April 4
Richter, Karl	Oct. 15
Richter, Sviatoslav	March 20
Riddle, Nelson	June 1
Ridout, Godfrey	May 6
Riley, Terry	June 24
Rimsky-Korsakov, Nicolai	March 18
Roach, Max	Jan. 10
Robeson, Paul	April 9
Robinson, "Smokey"	Feb. 19
Rochberg, George	July 5
Rodgers, Richard	June 28
Rogers, Bernard	Feb. 4
Rogers, Kenny	Aug. 21
Rollins, "Sonny"	Sept. 7
Romberg, Sigmund	July 29
Ronstadt, Linda	July 15
Rorem, Ned	Oct. 23
Rose, Leonard	July 27
Rosen, Charles	May 5
Rosenberg, Hilding	June 21
Ross, Diana	March 26
Rossini, Gioachino	Feb. 29
Rostropovich, Mstislav	March 27
Roussel, Albert	April 5
Rubinstein, Anton	Nov. 28
Rubinstein, Artur	Jan. 28
Ruggles, Carl	March 11
Rush, Tom	Feb. 8
Russell, Leon	April 2
Rydell, Bobby	April 26
Saint-Saëns, Camille	Oct. 9
Salieri, Antonio	Aug. 18
Santana, Carlos	July 20
Satie, Erik	May 17
Sax, Adolphe	Nov. 6
Scaggs, "Boz"	June 8
Scaria, Emil	Sept. 18
Scarlatti, Alessandro	May 2
Scarlatti, Domenico	Oct. 26
Scheidt, Samuel	Nov. 3
Schickele, Peter	July 17
Schiff, Andras	Dec. 21
Schippers, Thomas	March 9
Schirmer, Gustav	Sept. 19
Schnabel, Artur	April 17
Schnabel, Karl Ulrich	Aug. 6
Schnittke, Alfred	Nov. 24
Schoenberg, Arnold	Sept. 13
Schorr, Friedrich	Sept. 2
Schreier, Peter	July 29
Schreker, Franz	March 23
Schub, André-Michel	Dec. 26
Schubert, Franz	Jan. 31
Schuller, Gunther	Nov. 22
Schuman, William Howard	Aug. 4
Schumann, Clara	Sept. 13
Schumann, Elisabeth	June 13
Schumann, Robert	June 8
Schütz, Heinrich	Oct. 8
Schwarz, Gerard	Aug. 19
Schwarzkopf, Elisabeth	Dec. 9
Schweitzer, Albert	Jan. 14
Scimone, Claudio	Dec. 23
Scotto, Renata	Feb. 24
Scriabin, Alexander	Jan. 6

Scruggs, Earl	Jan. 6	Spiegel, Laurie	Sept. 20	Suppé, Franz von	April 18
Searle, Humphrey	Aug. 26	Spohr, Ludwig	April 5	Suter, Hermann	April 28
Sebastian, John	March 17	Springsteen, Bruce	Sept. 23	Sutherland, Dame Joan	Nov. 7
Sedaka, Neil	March 13	Squire, William		Suzuki, Shin'ichi	Oct. 18
Seeger, Pete	May 3	Barclay	Oct. 16	Svetlanov, Evgeny	Sept. 6
Segovia, Andrés	Feb. 21	Stamitz, Johann		Swanson, Howard	Aug. 18
Serkin, Peter	July 24	Wenzel	June 19	Szell, George	June 7
Serkin, Rudolf	March 28	Stanford, Sir Charles		Szeryng, Henryk	Sept. 22
Sessions, Roger	Dec. 28	Villiers	Sept. 30	Szymanowski, Karol	Oct. 6
Séverac, Déodat de	July 20	Stapp, Olivia	May 30		
Shankar, Ravi	April 7	Starker, Janos	July 5	**T**addei, Giuseppe	June 26
Shaw, Artie	May 23	Starr, Ringo	July 7	Tailleferre, Germaine	April 19
Shaw, Robert	April 30	Steber, Eleanor	July 17	Tajo, Italo	April 25
Shearing, George	Aug. 13	Steinway, Heinrich		Takemitsu, Toru	Oct. 8
Shifrin, Seymour	Feb. 28	Engelhard	Feb. 15	Tal, Josef	Sept. 18
Short, Bobby	Sept. 15	Stern, Isaac	July 21	Talma, Louise	Oct. 31
Shostakovich, Dmitri	Sept. 25	Stevens, Cat	July 21	Talvela, Martti	Feb. 4
Sibelius, Jean	Dec. 8	Stevens, Risë	June 11	Tatum, Art	Oct. 13
Siegmeister, Elie	Jan. 15	Stewart, Rod	Jan. 10	Tauber, Richard	May 16
Sills, Beverly	May 25	Stewart, Thomas	Aug. 29	Tausig, Carl	Nov. 4
Simionato, Giulietta	May 5	Still, William Grant	May 11	Tausinger, Jan	Nov. 1
Simon, Carly	June 25	Stills, Stephen	Jan. 3	Tavener, John	Jan. 28
Simon, Paul	Oct. 13	Stilwell, Richard	May 6	Taylor, Cecil	March 15
Simone, Nina	Feb. 21	Stockhausen,		Taylor, Deems	Dec. 22
Sims, "Zoot"	Oct. 29	Karlheinz	Aug. 22	Taylor, James	March 12
Sinatra, Frank	Dec. 12	Stoessel, Albert	Oct. 11	Taylor, Livingston	Nov. 21
Sinding, Christian	Jan. 11	Stokowski, Leopold	April 18	Tchaikovsky, Piotr	
Sinigaglia, Leone	Aug. 14	Stone, Sly	March 15	Ilyich	May 7
Sinopoli, Giuseppe	Nov. 2	Stookey, Paul	Nov. 30	Te Kanawa, Dame Kiri	March 6
Slezak, Leo	Aug. 18	Stout, Alan	Nov. 26	Telemann, Georg	
Slick, Grace	Oct. 30	Stradivari, Francesco	Feb. 1	Philipp	March 14
Slonimsky, Nicolas	April 27	Stratas, Teresa	May 26	Tennstedt, Klaus	June 6
Smetana, Bedřich	March 2	Strauss, Johann, Jr.	Oct. 25	Terry, "Sonny"	Oct. 24
Smith, Bessie	April 15	Strauss, Johann, Sr.	March 14	Thebom, Blanche	Sept. 19
Smith, Kate	May 1	Strauss, Richard	June 11	Thomas, Ambroise	Aug. 5
Smith, William O.	Sept. 22	Stravinsky, Igor	June 17	Thomas, Michael	
Smyth, Dame Ethel	April 22	Strayhorn, Billy	Nov. 29	Tilson	Dec. 21
Snow, Hank	May 9	Streicher, Johann		Thompson, Randall	April 21
Snow, Phoebe	July 17	Andreas	Dec. 13	Thomson, Virgil	Nov. 25
Söderström, Elisabeth	May 7	Streisand, Barbra	April 24	Tibbett, Lawrence	Nov. 16
Solti, Sir Georg	Oct. 21	Strouse, Charles	June 7	Tippett, Sir Michael	Jan. 2
Sondheim, Stephen	March 22	Subotnick, Morton	April 14	Toch, Ernst	Dec. 7
Sontag, Henriette	Jan. 3	Suk, Josef	Jan. 4	Tommasini, Vincenzo	Sept. 17
Sousa, John Philip	Nov. 6	Sullivan, Sir Arthur	May 13	Tomowa-Sintow, Anna	Sept. 22
Spaeth, Sigmund	April 10	Sumac, Yma	Sept. 10	Toscanini, Arturo	March 25